This bird's-eye panoramic view shows Norfolk and Portsmouth in 1873. Courtesy Sargeant Memorial Room, Kirn Memorial Library

PORTSMOUTH
a pictorial history
Alf J. and Ramona H. Mapp

This view of High Street was taken looking east from Court Street in 1950. Photo by Charles C. Wright, courtesy Portsmouth Public Library

PORTSMOUTH
a pictorial history
Alf J. and Ramona H. Mapp

THE DONNING COMPANY
PUBLISHERS
NORFOLK/VIRGINIA BEACH

380 years of history

Portsmouth: A Pictorial History carries the story of our community from 1608, when Capt. John Smith mapped its future site, to 1988 when major challenges and opportunities suggest that it may be on the threshold of a great new era. Although economic and cultural growth in the city is traced to 1988, the narrative of political events since 1984 is carried solely in pictures and captions, the events of the past four years being too recent to afford adequate perspective for detailed analysis.

Copyright © 1989 by Alf J. Mapp, Jr. and Ramona H. Mapp

All rights reserved, including the right to reproduce this work in any form whatsoever without permission in writing from the publisher except for brief passages in connection with a review. For information, write:
   The Donning Company/Publishers
   5659 Virginia Beach Boulevard
   Norfolk, Virginia 23502

Edited by Richard A. Horwege
Design by Sherri Faye Caldow

Library of Congress Cataloging-in-Publication Data
Mapp, Alf J. (Alf Johnson), 1925-
  Portsmouth: a pictorial history/by Alf J.
and Ramona H. Mapp.
    p.   cm.
  Bibliography: p.
  Includes index.
  ISBN 0-89865-750-4 (lim. ed.)
    1. Portsmouth (Va.)—History—Pictorial works.
2. Portsmouth (Va.)—Description—Views.
I. Mapp, Ramona H. II. Title.
F234.P8M36   1989   88-37364 975.5'522—dc19   CIP

Printed in the United States of America

contents

ACKNOWLEDGMENTS 9
PREFACE: Portsmouth: Junction of Past and Present 11
CHAPTER ONE: The Setting 13
CHAPTER TWO: Indians and Pioneers 19
CHAPTER THREE: Birth of Portsmouth 25
FEATURE SECTION: Houses of Worship 30
CHAPTER FOUR: The Revolution 43
CHAPTER FIVE: Peaceful Growth 51
CHAPTER SIX: Back to War 55
FEATURE SECTION: Portsmouth Schools 58
CHAPTER SEVEN: Rapid Progress 87
FEATURE SECTION: The Navy Yard 92
CHAPTER EIGHT: Pestilence and War 97
CHAPTER NINE: New Era 107
   Sidebar: City Managers of Portsmouth 111
CHAPTER TEN: World War I 135
FEATURE SECTION: Hospitals of Former Days 142
CHAPTER ELEVEN: Uneasy Peace 147
FEATURE SECTION: Police and Fire Departments 154
CHAPTER TWELVE: World War II 159
   Sidebar: First Citizens of Portsmouth 161
FEATURE SECTION: Trains 164
FEATURE SECTION: Sports 168
CHAPTER THIRTEEN: Mixed Signals 173
   Sidebar: Coast Guard 176
FEATURE SECTION: Storms 190
CHAPTER FOURTEEN: Stirrings of Progress 195
   Sidebar: Mayors of Portsmouth 197
FEATURE SECTION: Some Neighborhoods and Homes 208
CHAPTER FIFTEEN: The Future 215
APPENDIX: Portsmouth's National Notables 217
BIBLIOGRAPHY 221
INDEX 223
ABOUT THE AUTHORS 224

The Watts House, 516 North Street, built by Col. Dempsey Watts in 1799 and housing the Watts family until the mid-twentieth century, was the setting for some of Portsmouth's most distinguished gatherings. Chief Black Hawk was entertained here in 1820 and Henry Clay in 1844. Some ladies were pleased, and some disconcerted, by Clay's practice of kissing all female guests at the party in his honor.
Ramona H. Mapp photo

The Nivison-Ball-Albertson House, 417 Middle Street, was the scene of receptions for the Marquis de Lafayette in 1824 and President Andrew Jackson in 1833. Erected about 1784 at the intersection of Crawford and Glasgow Streets, the house was moved to its present location in 1869. The home is actually two stories high but the long dormers and peculiar roof style met legal requirements for a story-and-a-half house, allowing the original owners to qualify for a lower tax rate on their real estate. The building served as barracks for American troops in the War of 1812.
William J. Maloney photo

acknowledgments

Anyone producing a history of Portsmouth is indebted to four people whose contributions deserve more than routine inclusion in a bibliography. Miss Mildred Holladay, in the 1930s, preserved much traditional lore that she was heir to because of her youthful association with elderly citizens who had played leading roles in the community. J. Cloyd Emmerson and Marshall W. Butt, Sr., were indefatigable and scrupulous researchers into Portsmouth's history. Robert W. Wentz Jr., has literally rescued from the trash heap hundreds of irreplaceable photographs that let us know what the community and its citizens looked like in past decades.

Our gratitude to the Portsmouth Public Library is immense. The documentary and pictorial resources of its Virginia Room are rich in Portsmouth history and Brooke Butt Maupin, who presides over the collection, is herself not the least of those resources. Her knowledge, her detective skills, and her wholehearted cooperation have made this book a better one than it otherwise would have been. Dean Burgess, director of the Portsmouth Public Library, and Susan Burton, manager of the Main Branch Library, have been most helpful. William A. Brown III, assistant director of the Portsmouth Public Library, has made available findings from his extensive research on Portsmouth in the American Revolution.

Another institution that has been of great help is the Portsmouth Museum. Dr. Nancy Melton, museum director, and her staff have provided information and pictures. Especially helpful were Alice C. Hanes, Naval Shipyard Museum curator, and staff members Shelley L. Gluse and George C. Walker.

A. C. Hinton, coordinator of administrative services for Portsmouth Public Schools, supplied both pictures and information on school superintendents. Joe M. Law, Public Affairs Officer, Navy Yard, provided photographs and detailed information. Paul W. Parker, Jr., associate pastor at Court Street Baptist Church, provided valuable documents and pictures from his own materials and from the Court Street Bicentennial Collection. Petty Officer Steve Blondo, Fifth Coast Guard District, supplied photographs and a history of the Coast Guard in Portsmouth. And Capt. (Ret.) Theodore Conway, command historian, furnished slides and details of the Portsmouth Naval Hospital.

Many others have helped:

Lt. Dennis A. Mook, Sgt. J. R. Murray, Sgt. Ken Teller, Officer G. A. Brown and Barbara Pierce of the Portsmouth Police Department; Portsmouth Fire Chief Odell Benton; William J. Maloney, photographer; James E. Hall, photographer; Frankee Spurling, Portsmouth Parks and Recreation; Jack Milliner Photography; Richard Long, Photo Zone; Faith Stuart, Portsmouth Chamber of Commerce; Pamela Jones, Portsmouth Tourism coordinator; Louise DeVere, *Olde Times* magazine; Gloria O. Webb; Jack P. Barnes; Richard J. Davis; Allen Eckstine; Willard J. Moody; Ira J. Richardson; James E. Hall; Reed Rapoport; Richard and Donna Wood; Mrs. G. Robert House; Guy Morris; Zelma G. Rivin; Porter Hardy, Jr.; Richard E. Barnes; E. Anne Stokes; Marshall W. Butt, Jr.; Dr. Harvey N. Johnson, Jr.; Dorothy M. Hill; Jane Garrett; Joseph Pociask; James G. Norcom; Ben Foster, Sr.; Mary Brown Channel; J. E. Johansen; Eleanor Phillips Cross; Bruce Gill Murdaugh; Bertha Winborne Edwards; Gayle Atwood Channel; Diane Griffin; Ida Kay Jordan; Director Herbert J. Simpson and staff, Virginia Sports Hall of Fame; Maudie Young; Betty Etz; Audrey Orton; Alfred F. Marin; John Paul Hanbury; Barnabus (Billy) Baker; and Lawrence l'Anson.

Tidewater Community College, Portsmouth Campus; Portsmouth City Planning Office; Catherine Hatcher, historian, Monumental Methodist Church; Dr. Wasena F. Wright, Jr., pastor, Centenary Methodist Church; John E. Peters, Public Affairs Office, Atlantic Division, NAVFAC; Brooks Johnson, photography curator, The Chrysler Museum; Peggy Haile, assistant head librarian of the Sargeant Room, Norfolk Public Library; Virginia State Library; Lacy W. Dick, Valentine Museum, Richmond, Virginia.

Portions of the book have been adapted from two articles, "Bay Region Dwarfs Dreams" and "Norfolk County Ferries Face the Final Voyage," both by Alf J. Mapp, Jr., which appeared respectively in April 11, 1964 and August 14, 1955 issues of the *Virginian-Pilot*.

In addition to their other services, both Mary Brown Channel and Brooke Butt Maupin read our manuscript before publication, checking it against their encyclopedic knowledge of Portsmouth history.

Almost everyone approached has been quite helpful, some doing far more than could reasonably have been expected. If some individuals or organizations appear more often than comparable ones as examples within their categories, it is because of the zeal with which some brought forth helpful materials while others, because of modesty or absorption with other concerns, were not as forthcoming. All in all, the friendly interest and helpfulness of Portsmouth people has been a heartening reminder of one of the things that make our city a great community.

Alf J. Mapp, Jr.

Ramona H. Mapp

preface
PORTSMOUTH: JUNCTION OF PAST AND PRESENT

In a gray age of urban uniformity, Portsmouth—like New Orleans, San Francisco, and Charleston, South Carolina—is a glowing island of individuality. The Virginia city has its buildings of concrete, glass, and aluminum, and some are handsome examples of the genre. But the tone of its downtown area is set by warm colors—the mellow brick of sidewalks, public buildings, storefronts, and private homes dating from the eighteenth and nineteenth centuries. In summer a red and pink floral tide flows down the center of High Street toward the blue of the harbor and pours in peripheral streams down side streets.

Located on the world's greatest natural harbor and boasting a naval shipyard that is the nation's oldest and largest, Portsmouth is both enriched by a noble tradition and infused with the excitement of playing an important role in contemporary events. Block-long aircraft carriers and sleek atomic submarines, under the surveillance of eighteenth and nineteenth-century cannon, glide past shores passed by Spanish galleons in the 1580s and surveyed by Capt. John Smith in 1608.

A study by the American Institute of Architects has cited Portsmouth as having the largest concentration of architecturally noteworthy eighteenth and nineteenth-century dwellings anywhere on the East Coast between Georgetown and Alexandria on the north and Charleston, South Carolina on the south. Behind walls caressed by the shadows of old oaks and elms, Portsmouth people still tell anecdotes of the visits of Lafayette, Andrew Jackson, Henry Clay, Chief Black Hawk, Robert E. Lee, and the two Presidents Roosevelt.

They talk too of the achievements of Portsmouth people—some currently resident, some making history elsewhere—who now are national or international leaders in politics, diplomacy, business, scholarship, and the arts. A 1987 salute to Portsmouth notables drew national attention to the fact that in recent times the city has produced far more than its share of celebrities.

Though Portsmouth people take pride in these achievements and in such distinctions as receiving the National Bicentennial Medal and having Portsmouth named an All-America City, they delight even more in the recent restoration of its downtown area to the elegance and charm of former days, coupled with the burgeoning of cultural facilities and a diversity of sophisticated restaurants drawing visitors from many other communities.

The city that made international history when Cornwallis abandoned headquarters in Portsmouth to move on Yorktown, and again when the C.S.S. *Virginia (Merrimac)* met the *Monitor* in the great duel of ironclads, is once again part of the mainstream of national and international events. But its residents cherish even more the privilege of walking along sun-flecked brick walks under the blossoming glory of watermelon-pink crape myrtle, flanked by the white lace of dogwood and the flame of azaleas. They love gazing across sloping lawns to white sails on blue water framed by ancient oaks. And they delight in summer breezes as they walk at night on a seawall from which they see, against the backdrop of a sister city's amber lights, the silver, red, and green gleams from passing pleasure boats and ferries.

In the following pages, we shall tell, in words and pictures, Portsmouth's story as recorded in state and national annals and as remembered by those who have seen chapters of it unfold.

Trinity Episcopal Rectory, 340 Court Street (foreground) is a good example of the Bristol-built (or high basement) dwelling with the tradesman's entrance at basement level and the guest's entrance up a flight of stairs.
William J. Maloney photo

chapter one
THE SETTING

The map of downtown Portsmouth, Virginia, is strikingly like that of the old part of its sister city, Portsmouth, England. Central to the grid in each instance is a broad thoroughfare called High Street. Running parallel are King Street on the south and Queen Street on the north. Adjacent to the business area of each city is a historic shipyard now serving a great modern navy. Even the Bristol-built houses of the Virginia community, with their high basements and outside stairs to the second story, have their counterparts in the sister city and many another English seaport town.

But for all of its charming English characteristics, Portsmouth, Virginia, is clearly a city of the American South. The warm climate nurtures a profusion of azaleas and camellias. It also has encouraged the addition to some old houses of wrought iron piazzas and balconies reminiscent of New Orleans. Many of England's structures and institutions have been transplanted to Virginia's Portsmouth, but in a new soil and a new climate they have undergone significant changes. To understand the city we must see it in the context of its geography.

A glance at the map shows that any city built where Portsmouth stands should be indissolubly wedded to the sea. It is on the south side of Hampton Roads, the world's greatest natural anchorage, about midway of the great Atlantic Coast of the United States. It is far enough south in the temperate zone to be free of ice except for those few instances when a winter storm of heroic proportions makes history and legends. It is at the mouth of the James River, one of the great streams of the East Coast, and of Chesapeake Bay, the largest inlet on the nation's Atlantic littoral.

Portsmouth is also in Tidewater Virginia, a coastal plain embracing all of the Commonwealth where the tides rise and fall. To put it another way, Tidewater is everything in Virginia east of the fall line, which is marked by the cities of Alexandria, Fredericksburg, and Richmond and extends from the Potomac River to the North Carolina border. Some Hampton Roads residents occasionally forget that Tidewater Virginia extends far beyond the cities of Portsmouth, Suffolk, Chesapeake, Norfolk, Virginia Beach, Hampton, and Newport News, but proud Tidewater residents in the Northern Neck, the Middle Peninsula, and the Eastern Shore are quick to point out the error.

■

Tidewater Virginia (hatched area on map) is east of the Fall Line running from the Maryland border to the North Carolina border. Numerals indicate (1) The Peninsula, (2) Middle Peninsula, (3) Northern Neck, and (4) Eastern Shore. "Tidewater Virginia" is defined by Virginia statute.

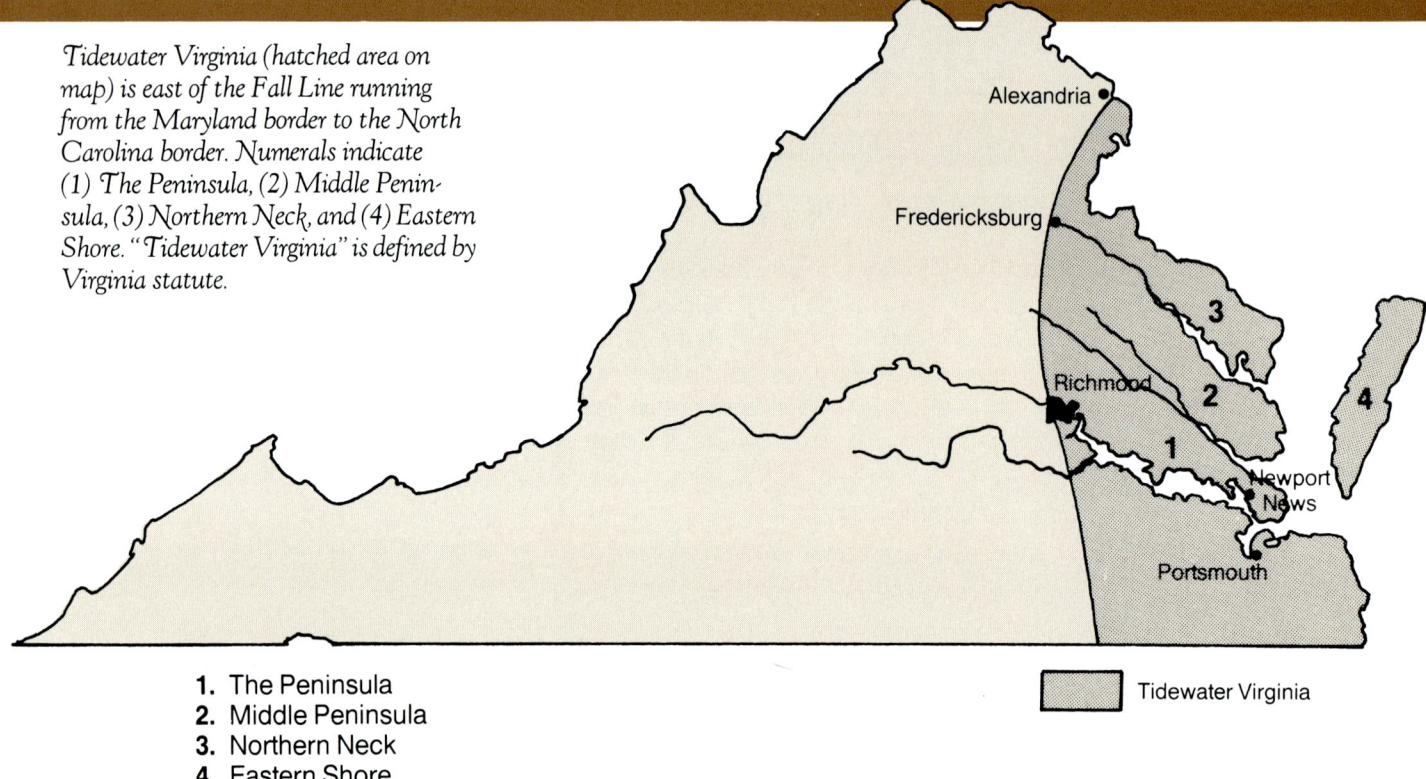

1. The Peninsula
2. Middle Peninsula
3. Northern Neck
4. Eastern Shore

Tidewater Virginia

Hampton Roads refers not only to the world's greatest harbor but also to the seven cities that border it: Virginia Beach, Chesapeake, Norfolk, Portsmouth, Suffolk, Newport News, and Hampton. The five cities on the southern side of the harbor constitute South Hampton Roads, or Southside Hampton Roads.

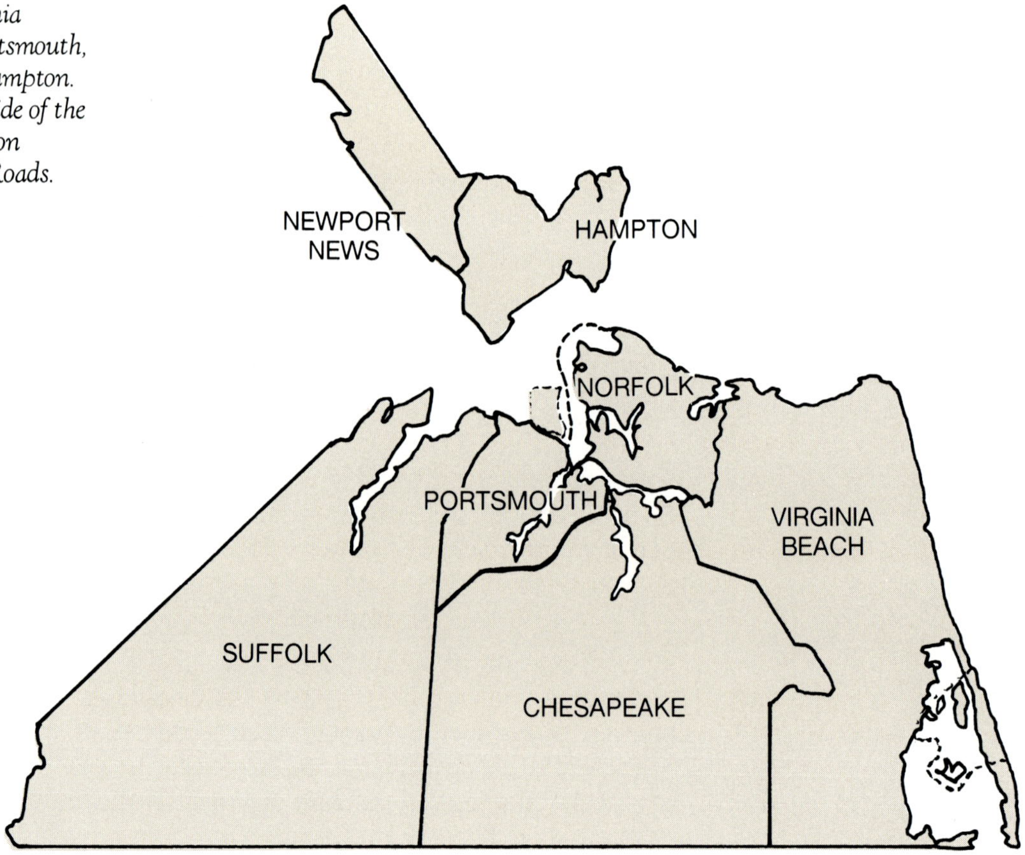

Tidewater Virginia

That portion of Virginia in which the tide rises and falls, i.e., all of Virginia east of the fall line, roughly marked by an imaginary line drawn from Alexandria on the Potomac to Fredericksburg on the Rappahannock to Richmond on the James and thence southward to the North Carolina line. Tidewater Virginia is bounded on the west by the fall line, on the north by the Maryland border, on the east by the Atlantic Ocean (Tidewater includes the two counties of the Eastern Shore of Virginia), and on the south by the North Carolina border.

Hampton Roads

(1) The harbor formed by the channel connecting the James, Nansemond, and Elizabeth rivers with Chesapeake Bay.
(2) The area composed of the cities of Norfolk, Portsmouth, Virginia Beach, Chesapeake, Suffolk, Newport News, and Hampton.

South Hampton Roads

The area composed of the cities of Norfolk, Portsmouth, Virginia Beach, Chesapeake, and Suffolk.

The Peninsula

When capitalized the name designates the Tidewater peninsula between the James and York rivers. It includes Williamsburg, Yorktown, Hampton, and Newport News.

Middle Peninsula

The Tidewater peninsula between the York and Rappahannock rivers.

Northern Neck

The Tidewater peninsula between the Rappahannock and Potomac rivers.

Eastern Shore

The Tidewater peninsula bounded on the north by the Maryland border, on the west by the Chesapeake Bay, and on the east by the Atlantic Ocean. It consists of the counties of Northampton and Accomac. The area to the north of the Eastern Shore of Virginia is known as the Eastern Shore of Maryland.

*Iron grillwork porches, fences, and balconies give many old Portsmouth homes a look reminiscent of New Orleans. One such residence (below) is on the northwest corner of London and Court streets, another on Glasgow Street.
Ramona H. Mapp photos*

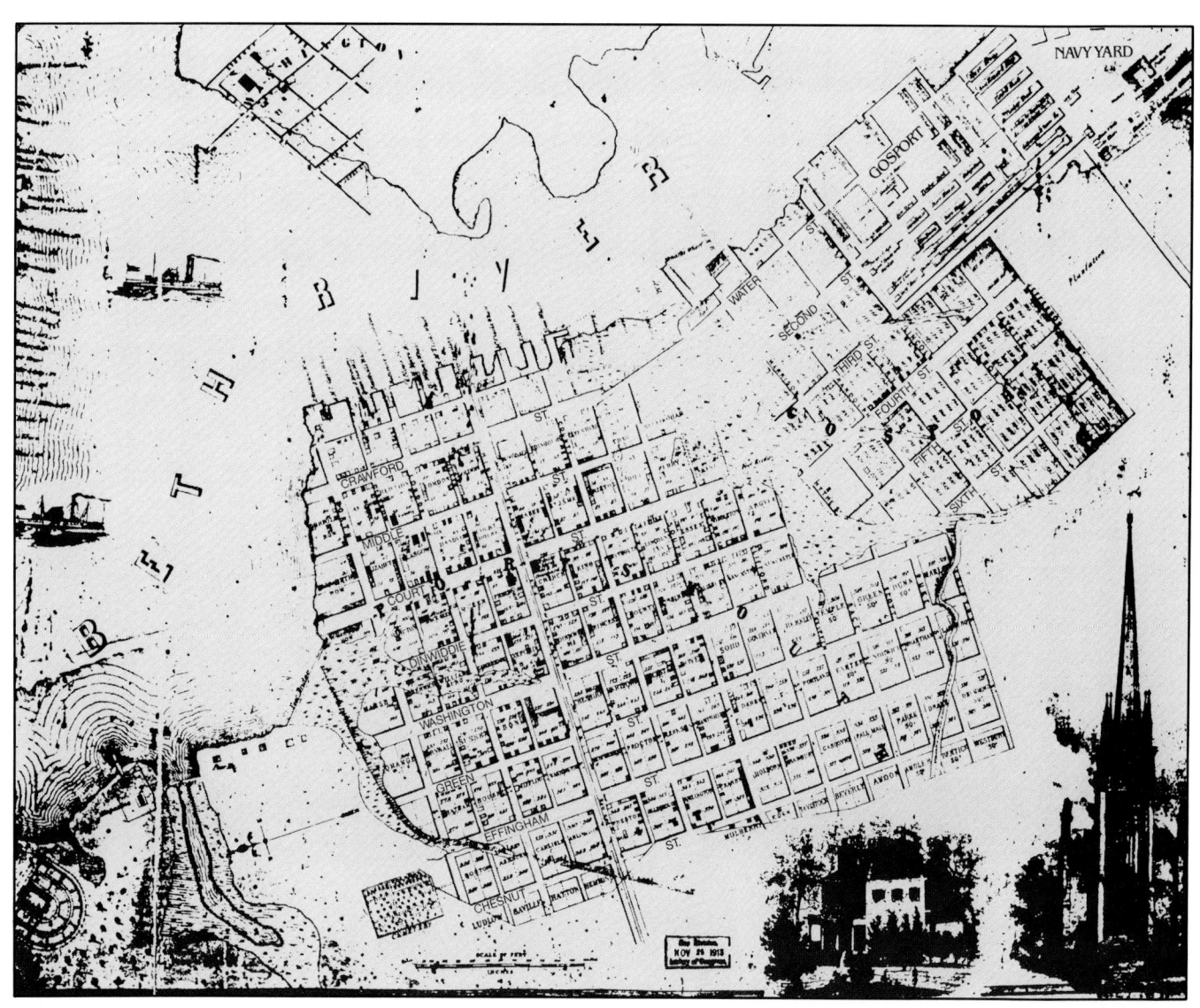

Rolin and Keily's 1851 map of Portsmouth shows the streets and squares as laid out by the town's founder, Colonel William Crawford, in 1752.

Captain John Smith, savior of the Virginia colony, who in 1608 mapped the future site of Portsmouth.

chapter two
INDIANS AND PIONEERS

Virginia, it has often been observed, is a state of mind as well as a state. The Virginia mind-frame was first formed in Tidewater.

Three small English ships in the spring of 1607 sailed through the Virginia capes and into world history. The English settlers on board sailed past the future site of Portsmouth on their way up the James River to found Jamestown, the first permanent English settlement in America. The lands now within Portsmouth's borders were part of the original Jamestown Colony.

Capt. John Smith, aboard one of the tiny vessels, reported that the Englishmen marveled much at the "mildness of the air, the fertility of the soil, . . .safe harbors, much merchantable fish, and places fit for . . .building of ships" and other industry.

Captain Smith was a bold adventurer and he dreamed of a "second Rome" on the shores of the Chesapeake. But if he could return today to the area which he observed so closely in 1607 and mapped so diligently in 1608, he might be struck dumb for once by a glimpse of the extent to which the potential for the shipbuilding and seafood industries and growth of cities has been realized. The *Susan Constant*, flagship of the 1607 expedition, would be dwarfed even by the propellers of great, gray naval vessels and black-hulled liners launched from the shipyards of Hampton Roads.

High-rise office buildings and apartments tower incomparably far above the "goodly tall trees" which one of Smith's colleagues said dwarfed Englishmen when they stepped ashore. The air which Smith admired for its mildness promoted the development of beaches where many thousands frolic, as tanned and almost as briefly clad as the Indians who greeted him.

And, in the upper reaches of that air, fighter planes and commercial airliners roar back and forth on their missions. Still higher, other jets—mere gleaming bits of metal—silently trace arabesques of white plume against the "central blue."

But Smith and his companions would not find change everywhere. The bay itself remains unmarked by the countless vessels that for fleeting instants have engraved white wakes across its waters. Parts of the Dismal Swamp, which extends into Portsmouth's neighboring city of Chesapeake, not only bear no marks of men but are still quite capable of swallowing up man himself. And white gulls, like those that wheel above Portsmouth's waterfront, wheel also above the shifting dunes of nearby Virginia Beach, screaming in a language at once as familiar and as alien to us as to Smith and, for that matter, to the first men and women who left their footprints in the tide-washed sands of the Chesapeake.

In fact, a good case can be made that the Chesapeake, despite human depredations, has left more marks on the people along its shores than they have left on the bay.

The Chesapeake had been molding men and women for centuries before the coming of the English in 1607. The life rhythm of the Indians was literally synchronized with the rise and fall of the tides in the Chesapeake and its tributaries. The great Indian Emperor Powhatan ruled over virtually all of Tidewater Virginia at the coming of the English. For generations his people, the Powhatans, a division of the great Algonquin tribes, had occupied the lands along the Potomac, Rappahannock, York, and James rivers and the creeks and inlets of the Eastern Shore. In the vicinity of the future city of Portsmouth were two tribes under Powhatan's influence if not always under his direct domination. They were the Chesapeakes, who lived between the Elizabeth River and the Atlantic Ocean, and the Nansemonds, who lived within Isle of Wight County and the present cities of Chesapeake and Suffolk.

The Powhatans were only partially an agricultural people. The survival of the population of nine thousand that Captain Smith found was dependent upon the bounty of the bay and rivers and upon land animals who, in their feeding habits, seemed mysteriously responsive to the ebb and flow of the tides.

The dwellings of the Tidewater Indians were not inferior to the huts of many European peasants of the same period. The teepees that dotted the Western plains and more recently have besprinkled hundreds of film sets were not characteristic of Hampton Roads or the Chesapeake area in general. Far more common were the arbor houses. Built on a framework of saplings placed in the ground at regular intervals in two parallel lines and tied together at the tops to form a tunnel vault, they were covered with bark shingles or with mats woven from the rushes of the bay or its tributaries. When the hide curtains were rolled down over the rectangular windows, each dwelling resembled a well-browned loaf of bread. The average one was twelve by eighteen feet.

Powhatan, as befitted a traveling potentate of many wives and much treasure, had a great many houses. One of these occupied more than three thousand square feet of floor space and remained the largest house in Virginia even after the erection of Gov. Sir William Berkeley's "Green Spring" mansion near Jamestown about 1646.

The problem of food was not so easily solved as that of shelter. Winters often brought scarcity. Contrary to what most people now would suspect, deer were not as plentiful in Virginia then as today, and felling smaller game with bow and arrow was not an easy task. Often the resources of the bay and the rivers made the difference between life and death. In frozen February as well as in the spring, sturgeon and herring were plentiful. The most dependable food of all was the oyster, and oyster roasts were favorite social events in Tidewater long before the coming of the English. Oystering was then unbelievably easy. No tonging was necessary. At low tide, tops of oyster beds rose above the water like islands. The Indians simply pulled their canoes alongside and raked in what they wanted.

Life for the first English settlers in 1607 was not very different from that of the Indians. The settlers' cabins were not the log structures generally associated with the name. They were wattle houses, woven of the sticks and reeds and osiers of the waterside and daubed with its mud. Food was even more of a problem for the English than for the aborigines, for the newcomers were not adept at snaring fish in specially built traps or spearing them by torchlight. Nor were they knowledgeable about supplementing their limited stores of grain with roots, herbs, nuts, and berries.

In the "starving time," the dreadful winter of 1609-1610, all but sixty of the nearly five hundred settlers in Virginia were wiped out. The corpses of slain Indians were dug up and greedily devoured by some of the less squeamish. One man was charged with murdering his wife and salting the body to preserve it for future meals.

But the colony did survive and grow, and by 1619 it was making history of national and even international significance. Three events have made it "Virginia's Red Letter Year."

In that year arrangements were made for the sending of one hundred English women to become wives of the settlers. They arrived in 1620 to the kind of welcome one may well imagine in a colony of English males who had seen few of their countrywomen since embarking for America. There is a mistaken but well entrenched belief that the Virginia planters bought their wives much as an Eastern sultan might purchase women for his harem. This misconception has arisen from the fact that each planter desiring to marry one of the women was required to pay the cost of her passage to Virginia. The women enjoyed independence of choice. They might reject any suitor not to their liking.

A ship bearing "20 and odd Negroes," the first brought to the mainland of what is now the United States, arrived in Tidewater Virginia in 1619. The popular assumption that they were slaves is understandable; they were so described in contemporary records. But the term "slave" was then used to designate indentured servants, persons who agreed to serve the colony or some of its subjects for designated periods in return for certain contracted benefits, such as a grant of land or the furnishing of certain tools for the pursuit of a trade.

The blacks who came in 1619 were laborers, but some indentured servants who came to Virginia performed secretarial or clerical tasks, and before the end of the seventeenth century some were tutors in Latin and Greek. No particular stigma was attached to their service. Some eventually became members of the colonial legislature.

As strangers to the prevalent culture, ignorant of the English language and markedly different physically from the English settlers, the blacks were particularly disadvantaged. No one can point to a particular day in Tidewater history when slavery was introduced. By the latter part of the seventeenth century, indenture had become slavery for many Negroes. The first Virginia planter officially recognized as a slaveowner was Anthony Johnson of Northampton County. Surprisingly, Johnson himself was a black who had completed his own indenture by about 1625. Before being given legal recognition in Virginia, slavery had been declared legal in Conecticut.

The third great event of 1619 in Tidewater Virginia was the convening at Jamestown of the General Assembly, the first representative legislature in the New World, and today in the English-speaking world second to the British Parliament. Borrowing heavily from English experience and adapting old customs to the exigencies of New World conditions, the Virginia lawmakers established precedents that govern most American legislatures, including the Congress of the United States, to this day. Theirs was a bicameral assembly. The House of Burgesses, as the lower chamber was called, had a speaker, a chaplain, a clerk, and a sergeant at arms. The assembly established its right to judge the qualifications of its own members and set the principle of denying representation to those enjoying special privileges.

On December 4, 1619, before Plymouth Rock had felt "the stern, impassioned stress" of a Pilgrim foot, Virginians at Berkeley Hundred on the James River observed the first Thanksgiving in America. A commemorative celebration is held there every year, but for most Americans the view is blocked by a large Pilgrim hat in the foreground of their imaginations.

The Tidewater settlers had survived—in itself an accomplishment warranting celebration. But they had done more. They had taken a big step toward self govern-

Discovery, *reproduction of the ship of the same name that, with* Susan Constant *and* Godspeed, *brought to Virginia in 1607 the founders of the first permanent English settlement in America. The vessel shown under construction was built in West Norfolk, now part of Portsmouth, as a feature of the celebration in 1957 of the 350th anniversary of Jamestown.*
Photo courtesy Portsmouth Public Library

ment, something rare in the history of the world.

Less than three years after the red letter year of 1619, in which Virginians celebrated their triumph over starvation and disease, the colony was almost destroyed by another force. Disaster struck on March 22, 1622.

By then, peace between the settlers and the Indians had caused the English to lower their guard. The Indians enjoyed easy access to the settlers' homes and had been furnished with firearms so that they might provide more game for the white man's table.

Despite appearances, the Powhatans had never become reconciled to the English intrusion. Chief Powhatan himself was dead and in his place now was the wily Opecancanough. He plotted against the settlers a synchronized attack along the longest front for zero hour operations that America was to know until the Civil War. The Indians—some working in the fields beside the English, some seated in English homes—dealt death blows to any whites in sight at the moment that the position of the sun proclaimed the hour of 8:00 a.m. Some planters beat off their assailants. Several women used boiling water to great advantage. Nevertheless, nearly one-third of all whites in Virginia were killed.

The results would have been even more disastrous if Chanco, an Indian youth befriended by one of the planters, had not resolved his conflicting loyalties by warning his benefactor, who carried the word to Jamestown.

The vitality of the recovering colony was such that by 1634 it had five thousand members. They were so spread out that it was necessary to create eight counties, each with its own court of law, so that justice within reasonable traveling distance would be available to all people. Population growth on the south side of Hampton Roads lagged behind that elsewhere in the James River basin and on the Eastern Shore. But in 1636 growth was sufficient to split Elizabeth City County, the one that straddled Hampton Roads. The southern part was named New Norfolk. Within its borders, in the same year, a ferry service was established across the Elizabeth River. Eventually it connected the future cities of Norfolk and Portsmouth. When it was discontinued in 1955, after 319 years, it was cited as "the nation's oldest transportation line in continuous service." Residents of the area rejoiced in 1983 when ferry traffic between the two cities was resumed as a pleasant and colorful alternative to the tunnels.

Further population growth justified division of New Norfolk in 1637 into the counties of Lower Norfolk (embracing the future cities of Norfolk, Portsmouth, and Chesapeake) and Upper Norfolk (embracing the future city of Suffolk).

A series of agricultural misfortunes, the widening gap between small farmers and great planters, resentment of tyrannical acts of Gov. Sir William Berkeley, and impatience for decisive action against hostile Indians all culminated in 1676 in Bacon's Rebellion. An eloquent and charismatic young aristocrat, Nathaniel Bacon, became the leader of rebel forces that attacked the Indians and eventually the government itself, leaving Jamestown a smoking ruin. The governor had to flee to the Eastern Shore, which had been spared conflict with the Indians, and where many people were friendly to him. When Bacon died of a fever in October, the rebel movement lost impetus and direction. The governor soon triumphed. He ordered the hanging of every one of Bacon's lieutenants who could be captured. Tearful pleas from grief-crazed wives—even if sobbed out on bended knee—were ignored.

Bacon's Rebellion, fought in the name of liberty exactly a century before the Declaration of Independence, is sometimes called the "false dawn" of American independence. Though some condemn Bacon as a rabble rouser and consider his lieutenants irresponsible adventurers, more Americans in the generations since have hailed them as heroes of democracy.

■

Powhatan in his lodge was pictured on the upper left of Captain Smith's map of Virginia. The figure of a stalwart Indian warrior decorated the upper right corner of Smith's map.
Courtesy Virginia Historical Society

Governor Sir William Berkeley, who hanged Captain William Carver, owner of land on which Portsmouth would be built.
Picture courtesy Virginia Historical Society

chapter three
BIRTH OF PORTSMOUTH

The fate of one of Nathaniel Bacon's lieutenants played a key role in the founding of Portsmouth. A master mariner and merchant who added planter to his occupations after arriving in New Norfolk County sometime before 1657, Capt. William Carver grew in prosperity and in the regard of his neighbors. Ironically, in the light of Carver's eventual role as a rebel, he was praised by Governor Berkeley as "a valiant man and stout seaman." Several successive land grants increased the captain's estate to more than sixteen hundred acres. The governor appointed him a justice of the county. Later Carver was elected to the House of Burgesses. In 1670 he became high sheriff, the most important executive officer, of Lower Norfolk County.

A dinner that Carver attended in 1672 changed his career. Sitting next to him was one Thomas Gilbert. Whether there had been earlier quarrels between the two men, we do not know. We know only that, in the course of the meal, Carver suddenly plunged a knife into Gilbert. The wound was fatal.

So Carver, both a justice and a respected law-enforcement officer, was tried for murder before the General Court of Virginia. He testified that he had no recollection of the crime "nor of any other action that day nor several days before or after." The court accepted this plea of temporary insanity and he was acquitted. Governor Berkeley, however, removed him from his position as justice.

Four years later, Nathaniel Bacon was leading a rebellion against Berkeley, and Carver was one of the rebel's most trusted officers. When the governor fled to the Eastern Shore, Bacon placed the veteran mariner in command of a ship and ordered him to proceed across Chesapeake Bay to keep a watch on Sir William.

The governor, secure in the midst of staunch supporters, tried to entice the captain ashore with promises of substantial rewards if he would desert Bacon. Carver replied that even "if he served the Devil he would be true to his trust."

Berkeley seized Carver's ship and the captain himself. Three or four days later Carver danced out his life at the end of a hangman's rope.

As the captain had been executed as a traitor, his lands reverted to the Crown. These included an 890-acre tract on the west side of the Elizabeth River. In 1691 Lower Norfolk County was further divided into Norfolk County and Princess Anne (the future Virginia Beach); the Carver property was within Norfolk County. In 1716 this parcel, with 239 additional acres was granted to William Crawford. In those days, many people agreed with Andrew Jackson's later dictum, "Damn a man who can't spell a word but one way." Crawford's name sometimes was spelled "Craford" or "Crafford." We may assume that the pronunciation was consistently the phonetic one suggested by "Crawford."

Like his ill-fated predecessor, the colonel was a prosperous merchant and shipowner who became a planter and served as justice, burgess, and high sheriff. He also became lieutenant colonel of the county militia. Part of his land, projecting into the Western Branch of the Elizabeth River opposite the town of Norfolk, became known as Crawford's Point. A successor to the ferry operated by Adam

Thorogood (Thoroughgood, Thorowgood) in 1636 plied between the two locations.

Crawford's chief claim to fame is what he did with sixty-five acres of his plantation. In 1752 he engaged Gershom Nimmo, the county surveyor, to lay off the area in streets and half-acre lots. The enabling act passed by the General Assembly of Virginia provided that the new community should be known as Portsmouth.

Portsmouth, England, was Crawford's hometown. He foresaw that the new town, like its Old World namesake, could become an important port and naval center.

Crawford was so confident of Portsmouth's future that he laid out High Street, its main thoroughfare, as a six-lane avenue stretching westward from the Elizabeth River. It was flanked by Queen and King streets, as was High Street in Portsmouth, England. Other parallel streets were named North, Glasgow, London, County, Crab, and South. North and South streets marked respectively the northern and southern bounds of the new community.

The east end of North Street was the Portsmouth terminal of the Elizabeth River ferry. Intersecting High Street not far from the river was Crawford Street, a north-south thoroughfare which the colonel named for himself. His own home was on the southeast corner of the intersection. Moving westward, the next street parallel to Crawford was Middle. Then came Court Street. The four corners of High and Court were assigned respectively to a courthouse, a market, a jail, and a church. No jail stands there now, but three of those corners are occupied by a courthouse (converted to a museum), a retail store, and a church.

The British origins of Portsmouth's founder were illustrated in the names of most of the town squares: Norfolk, Red Lion, London, Golden, Bloomsbery, Edinburg, Cavendish, Crab, Buckingham, Elizabeth, Glasgow, Hanover, Court House, Market, St. James, Bristol, Middle, Ferry, Kent, Hampton, Back Creek, Queen, Prison, Church, King, Portsmouth, Lincoln's Inn, Essex, Middleton, and Argyle.

Nine lots were sold in the first year, seventy-four in the first decade.

Portsmouth quickly assumed the maritime character of its English prototype. Wharves multiplied. Marshall Butt reported in *Portsmouth Under Four Flags*: "According to the vocations given in their deeds more than three-fourths of Portsmouth's first lot owners were engaged in or connected with the maritime trade either as merchants or craftsmen. Seventeen named themselves as merchants. These important men were generally shipowners or factors who built wharves and warehouses and traded by sea beyond the local level and whose business gave employment to others associated with ships and shipping. Next in number were the craftsmen who built and repaired the square-rigged sailing vessels ranging in size from those that navigated the rivers and inland waters to the tall-masted ships and brigs that sailed the seas."

Such entrepreneurs came mostly from Norfolk and from various counties of Southeastern Virginia. But some came from afar. Notable among them was Henry Wells, a celebrated carver of ships' figureheads, who left Philadelphia and set up shop on the Portsmouth waterfront.

In the forefront of Portsmouth maritime activities, as in those of Norfolk and the other Atlantic ports, were the Scottish merchants. At times they seemed almost to control the trade between Virginia and the mother country. Easily the foremost of this energetic breed in Portsmouth was Andrew Sprowle who in the year of Portsmouth's founding bought three lots at the intersection of Crawford and King streets. His holdings increased, steadily marching across town until they leaped over Crab Creek and included a large part of a satellite village. The village early came to be called Gosport. That was the name of a community in an analogous position to Portsmouth, England. The English Gosport was the site of a famous naval shipyard. Sprowle became the sole proprietor of Virginia's Gosport and on it he built a shipyard which served not only merchant vessels but also the British Navy. This establishment was awe-inspiring to many colonists. A contemporary reported that the principal structure was "a large warehouse built with stone, 91 feet in length, and 41 feet wide, 5 stories high, 3 of stone, and 2 of wood; the doors and windows, with a broad stairs of hewn stone, mostly brought from Britain at great expense." There were three other large warehouses and four additional buildings.

■

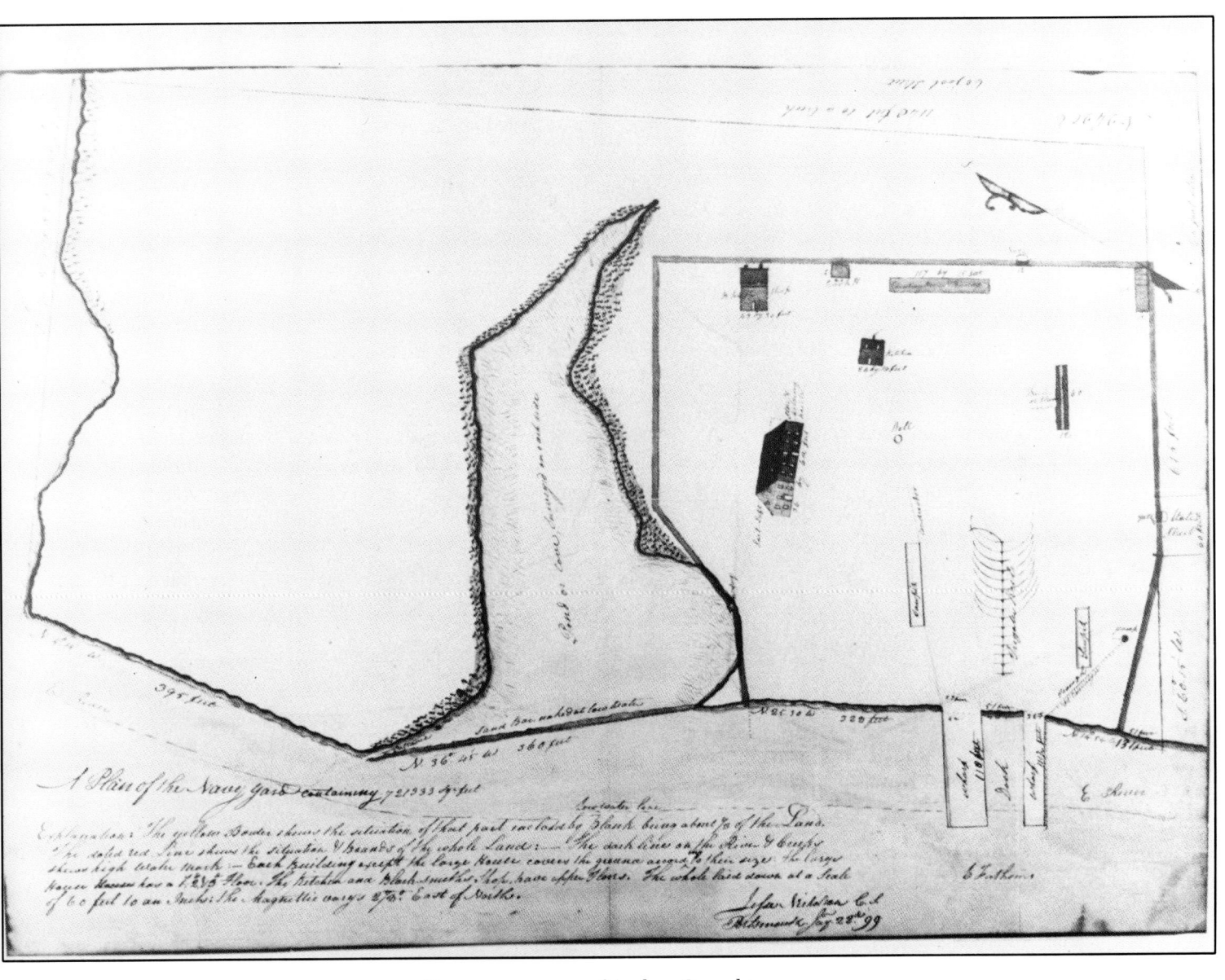

*Contemporary map of Andrew Sprowle's Gosport Shipyard.
Courtesy Portsmouth Naval Shipyard Museum*

Crawford Street, which Portsmouth's founder, Colonel William Crawford, named for himself. The basement of the Murdaugh house (left), on the northwest corner of Crawford and London streets, was seized by the provost marshal for his headquarters during Federal occupation of Portsmouth in the Civil War. Any Portsmouth resident who wished to go beyond the boundaries of the city had to obtain a pass from his office. In a few instances someone on duty would insist on exercising the right of search before granting a permit. The building became known as the Pass House.
William J. Maloney photo

Reed House, Swimming Point, apparently was built by Colonel Crawford to house the manager of his plantations. William J. Maloney photo

Red Lion Tavern, on London Street, has been converted to law offices. Its name was derived from its location on Red Lion Square, one of the squares into which Colonel Crawford divided Portsmouth. William J. Maloney photo

houses of worship

As in most American communities, churches and synagogues in Portsmouth have been social and educational as well as religious institutions. Sometimes they have also been political forces.

Trinity Episcopal Church, on the southwest corner of High and Court streets is Portsmouth's oldest house of worship. A Virginia State Historical Marker (left foreground) relates that the church was "built in 1762 as the parish church of Portsmouth Parish, established in 1761. Later named Trinity; enlarged in 1829; remodeled in 1893."
William J. Maloney photo

Two of Portsmouth's oldest churches are linked in this dramatically beautiful photograph taken from Trinity Parish House on December 15, 1958, after storms brought 14½ inches of snow, an unusual occurrence in the area. The camera looks across Trinity Churchyard to the First Presbyterian Church, built in 1877. Silhouetted against the snow and the light (left) is a cruciform monument to the first vestry of Portsmouth Parish: Thomas Grimes, Thomas Creech, James Ives, John Ferebee, thomas Veale, William Crawford, George Veale, John Tatem, John Herbert, Giles Randolph, Richard Carney, and Jeremiah Creech. Crawford, Portsmouth's founder gave the land on which the church was built. Marshall W. Butt, Sr., Portsmouth historian, noted in the 1940s that the Rev. John H. Wingfield, rector in 1821, had listed Barnaby Carney instead of Richard Carney as a member of the 1761 vestry. He suggested that, as Richard and Barnaby were brothers, the apparent discrepancy might result from a sibling's having been appointed to replace a man unable to complete his term.

Mt. Herman Baptist Temple has been a force for stability in a neighborhood that has experienced spectacular renewal.
Ramona H. Mapp photo

Portsmouth had originally been part of Elizabeth River Parish, centered in Norfolk. Portsmouth Parish was created by an act of the Virginia General Assembly in March 1761 to grant relief to Portsmouth and Norfolk County residents from a Norfolk vestry adjudged "guilty of some illegal practices oppressive to the inhabitants thereof." The Portsmouth Parish Vestry was chosen in obedience to the assembly's order that the sheriff of Norfolk County supervise balloting to "elect twelve of the most able and discreet persons." In those days, vestries directed certain functions of civil government as well as dealing with ecclesiastical matters.
Mike Williams photo courtesy Portsmouth Public Library

A much earlier picture of Trinity shows a steeple very different in design from the Romanesque Revival tower that now rises by the side of the sanctuary. Said to have been painted before 1858 by Margaret Collins, copy furnished to the authors by Barnabus W. Baker.

*Monumental United Methodist Church was founded by Virginia's first Methodist Society, organized in Portsmouth on November 14, 1772. Monumental's claim to be the oldest Methodist congregation in the South has gone unrefuted for many years. Its first house of worship, at South and Effingham streets, was replaced in 1792 by one on the south side of Glasgow Street between Court and Dinwiddie. Removal to the present site, on the southwest corner of Dinwiddie and Queen streets, was in 1831. That church burned in 1864 while held by Federal occupation forces. A temporary chapel was built in 1866. The present church (shown here), the congregation's fifth home, was completed in 1876.
Photo courtesy Catherine Hatcher, church historian*

*Before 1877 the congregation of Court Street Presbyterian Church worshipped at Middle Street Presbyterian Church, erected in 1872 at the northwest corner of London and Middle streets. This church burned, as had its predecessor, built on the same site in 1821.
Photo courtesy of Portsmouth Public Library*

The Byzantine Romanesque architecture of Court Street Baptist Church, erected in 1901 on the northeast corner of Court and Queen streets, is one of the most distinctive landmarks of downtown Portsmouth. Its predecessor on the same site was a neoclassical structure built 1838-1842 (below) and occupied during the Civil War by Federals who used it as a hospital. Its forerunner was a wooden structure erected in 1800. Organized on September 7, 1789, the congregation at first was known as the Norfolk and Portsmouth Baptist Church and met in Portsmouth homes. Norfolk members later withdrew to found a church more convenient to their homes. The first pastor was Rev. Thomas Armistead, a retired Army officer.
Photo of the Romanesque tower by Paul W. Parker, Jr.; the other from the Court Street Bicentennial Collection

The 1846 Court House is seen from Trinity Churchyard on January 10, 1962. Tombs include those of Commodore James Barron and other heroes of the early republic. Inscriptions, some quite long, range from the quaint to the deeply moving. The oldest stone commemorates Alexander Scot, who died January 1763 in his thirty-eighth year.
J. T. McClenny photo courtesy Portsmouth Public Library

Churchland Baptist Church, organized in 1785, was the mother congregation of Court Street Baptist Church and of many other churches in the Portsmouth area. The first building was erected at Shoulder's Hill, now the intersection of the old Suffolk Highway and Bennett's Creek Road, and was known as Shoulder's Hill Church. In 1829 a second sanctuary was erected on Sycamore Hill in Churchland. In 1840 the church changed its name to Churchland Baptist Church. The present building was dedicated in May 1963. In 1974 a Churchland native and son of the church, the Reverend Dr. Carney Hargroves, was elected president of the Baptist World Alliance, the international organization of Baptist congregations.
William J. Maloney photo

Centenary Methodist Church lifts its spire amid the pines on Cedar Lane in Churchland. The present structure was built in two stages, one completed in 1959 and the other in 1965. The congregation met in private homes before purchasing a building site in 1785. The first church burned and was replaced in 1848 with a new one called Wesley Chapel. In 1883 it was remodeled and its name was changed to Centenary "in anticipation of the congregation's centennial year." When this building and its site were outgrown, the church acquired its six-acre site on Cedar Lane. Photo courtesy Centenary Methodist Church

The "Blessing of the Animals" has become an annual tradition of Trinity Episcopal Church. At right in this 1965 photo is the Reverend C. Charles Vache, then rector. In 1978 he became Bishop of the Diocese of Southern Virginia. Mike Williams photo courtesy Portsmouth Public Library

Originally Central Methodist Church, this building at 519 County Street was acquired by Gomley Chesed Synagogue in 1901 and served as a temple until its sale to the Knights of Columbus in the 1950s. The congregation was founded in 1886 by Russian immigrants who opened their first synagogue, on High Street between Green and Effingham streets, in 1893.
Ramona H. Mapp photo

St. Paul's Catholic Church, at the northeast corner of High and Washington streets, is a cathedral-like building whose verdigris-covered copper-plated spire can be seen for miles. The present St. Paul's, the fifth to occupy this site, was built 1898-1905. Its immediate predecessor was erected 1865-1868.
William J. Maloney photo

Emmanuel African Methodist Episcopal Church, 637 North Street, is the oldest black church in Portsmouth. It traces its origins to a meeting house on South Street in 1772. In early times, as again in more recent years, blacks worshiped with whites in Methodist, Baptist, Presbyterian, and Episcopal churches. The present structure was built in 1857 by a congregation consisting largely of slaves and free blacks.
Ramona H. Mapp photo

St. John's Episcopal Church, on the northwest corner of London Boulevard and Washington Street, was organized in 1848 because of a doctrinal division in Trinity Church. An addition to the church was designed by the first licensed female architect in Virginia, Mary Brown Channel, daughter of the late Right Reverend William Ambrose Brown, Bishop of the Diocese of Southern Virginia and one-time rector of the church. The window over the communion table is a Tiffany one of superb quality.
William J. Maloney photo

The Reverend Ruth Mayhall talks with young friends at the Wesley Community Center.
Photo courtesy Portsmouth Public Library

Gomley Chesed Synagogue now stands at 3110 Sterling Point Drive in Churchland. The groundbreaking for this building was on November 21, 1954.
William Maloney photo

Ebenezer Baptist Church was designed by its versatile pastor, the Reverend Dr. Harvey N. Johnson, Sr., who was also a professional architect (1). The minister stands before the double doors of his unfinished church in a 1947 photo (2).

The building was completed in 1949. Since that time additions have been made in the rear. At the lectern, Dr. Johnson speaks in May 1969 at the dedication of Ebenezer Plaza, a fifty-two-unit townhouse development conceived by him (3). Full-church-front photo by William Maloney; the two in which Dr. Johnson appears are courtesy Harvey N. Johnson, Jr.

Zion Baptist Church, 527 Green Street, was organized on this site on March 10, 1865. The present edifice dates from 1895 and was remodeled in 1964. It is one of the oldest black churches in Portsmouth.
Ramona H. Mapp photo

Pentecostal Holiness Bishop Charles A. Twine (left) is honored April 1, 1960, on his one hundredth birthday in ceremonies attended by Mayor Barnabas W. (Billy) Baker and Judge Robert MacMurran (right).
Photo from the Rodgers Collection, Portsmouth Public Library

Commodore Richard Dale, second in command to John Paul Jones in the famous battle between Serapis *and the* Bonhomme Richard, *was Portsmouth's most prominent Revolutionary hero. In 1795-96 he returned to his hometown as commander of the Navy Yard. Immensely popular, he was described as an honest man "well up in all the little courtesies of life." According to Miss Mildred Holladay, his teachers recalled that "his daring and recklessness in spelling was only surpassed by his boldness in the fray." Photo courtesy Portsmouth Naval Shipyard Museum*

chapter four
THE REVOLUTION

Sprowle's establishment was the ancestor of the present Norfolk Naval Shipyard in Portsmouth, the principal federal facility of the kind in the United States. In Sprowle's time, as in the twentieth century, the Yard was noted for its giant crane. The one set up by the Scotsman was imported from London and was an iron machine with brass wheels and pulleys.

As Sprowle increased in prosperity he replaced his first home in Portsmouth with a large, three-story house with stone foundations, stone chimneys, and broad stone stairs leading to an expansive gallery swept by Elizabeth River breezes.

Portsmouth residents were amused by the contrast between the handsome condition of Sprowle's dwelling and place of business and his own shopworn personal appearance. They didn't know whether to attribute to carelessness or parsimony the fact that this rich citizen walked the streets of Portsmouth in stockings with holes in them.

The importance of Portsmouth marine facilities to the British Army and Navy became apparent in March 1755 during the French and Indian War when troop transports arrived in Portsmouth. The men aboard were assigned to Maj. Gen. Edward Braddock, recently appointed commander of all British forces opposed to the French in North America. The general's aide-de-camp was a Tidewater native, twenty-three-year-old Lt. Col. George Washington. The young officer wrote his brother: "I shall serve this campaign agreeably enough, as I am thereby freed from all commands but his (General Braddock's), and give orders to all, which must be implicitly obeyed."

But the campaign did not prove agreeable to Washington or anyone else in Braddock's force. Unwilling to abandon the tactics of European battlefields for those more appropriate to the American wilderness, the British general was defeated and fatally wounded at Monongahela, future sight of Pittsburg. Only Washington's leadership prevented the retreat from becoming a rout.

Washington was commissioned a full colonel and made commander-in-chief of Virginia forces. In 1756 clothing and equipment for his troops were imported through Portsmouth.

The coming of the American Revolution posed hard choices for some Portsmouth residents. Their location exposed them to the British Navy's guns and their lifeline of commerce tied them to Britain.

Portsmouth's founder was spared the necessity for such a decision. He died in 1762. The town's next most prominent citizen had no trouble making up his mind. His patriotic regard for his native land was augmented by his profits from commerce with Britain and work for the Royal Navy. Andrew Sprowle was an ardent Tory.

The royal governor of Virginia in 1775 was John Murray, earl of Dunmore, viscount Fincastle, baron of Blair, of Moulin, and of Tillymount. He shared the divine rights philosophy of his royal Stuart ancestors. In the past year, plagued with repeated challenges from the House of Burgesses, Dunmore had often tossed his auburn head in anger and his brown eyes had flashed fire. By October, revolutionary companies from eight counties had camped outside Williamsburg, which had succeeded Jamestown as the colonial capital. For orders they looked to a newly organized Committee of Safety which claimed to be the true government of Virginia. The Old Dominion's leaders already had met with those of sister colonies in a Continental Congress at Philadelphia.

Dunmore had some troops at his disposal, but the country was rising against him. He still commanded the only naval force in Virginia. With it he fled to Portsmouth where he became Sprowle's guest at the Gosport Shipyard. From there Dunmore commanded his navy and sent orders to followers elsewhere in the colony. Thus Gosport, the satellite village later absorbed by Portsmouth, was briefly the royal capital of Virginia. Popular report had the governor "living riotously" upon his host's resources but his lordship wryly styled himself "Lieutenant-Governor of Gosport."

Residents of Hampton Roads were in a miserable situation, living in the shadow of Dunmore's guns and at the same time fearful that Virginia troops would torch their towns to deprive the royalists of bases. About 4:00 a.m. on New Year's Day 1776 Dunmore trained the seventy guns of his fleet on Norfolk. Portsmouth citizens, waked by the fearful cannonade, looked across the Elizabeth River and saw the docks of the sister city in flames. The incendiaries were parties sent ashore from the governor's ships.

By the next night, fires were reduced to embers, but four-fifths of Norfolk's buildings had been destroyed. A few weeks later the remaining structures, with the exception of St. Paul's Church, were burned on orders of the Committee of Safety, which had had them appraised to determine fair compensation for the owners. Washington, now commander of the Continental Army, rejoiced that the burning of Norfolk had not only deprived the Royal Navy of a valuable base and provisioning center but also had eradicated a nest of Tories.

The fate of Norfolk, coupled with defeat of the governor's troops at Great Bridge in Norfolk County, convinced his lordship to entrench his forces on Hospital Point in Portsmouth and await reinforcements from New York. Among the Americans most conspicuous for gallantry at Great Bridge was William Flora, a free black from Portsmouth.

Tories from Portsmouth and Norfolk County were so helpful in supplying food to Dunmore that the Committee of Safety instructed Gen. Charles Lee to propose a

Lord Dunmore, Virginia's last royal governor, who, after his flight from Williamsburg, made Portsmouth temporarily the royal capital of Virginia. Picture courtesy Virginia Historical Society

solution. General Lee was a crane-like figure followed everywhere by a pack of dogs. His eccentricity was equaled by his arrogance. He shocked the committee by replying that he had already dealt with the problem without consulting civilian authority. He had destroyed the homes of Sprowle and at least two other Portsmouth Tories. He had destroyed most of the wharves and waterfront warehouses of the town and had burned two merchant ships. He had gone so far as to force an evacuation of Portsmouth and disclosed that he had barely suppressed his desire to burn it "totally."

Though warning that he must in future be more regardful of civilian authority, the Committee replied, "When we reflect on the several reasons by you assigned for your proceedings at Portsmouth, we much approve of the whole of your conduct to those people." In the American colonies as a whole, about one-third of the people supported the rebel cause, while one-third were loyal to the royal government, and the remaining third were not passionately involved with either camp. But the Tories were especially bold in communities such as those of Hampton Roads which lived under the guns of the Royal Navy.

General Lee's harsh measures in Portsmouth, the outbreak of smallpox among Dunmore's black troops, and reports of an impending rebel attack in strength caused the Governor to abandon Hampton Roads for Gwynn's Island, taking Sprowle with him. On August 7, 1776, he sailed from Virginia to a refuge in New York, leaving Sprowle behind in a grave on the island.

The Fourth Virginia Regiment was posted to Portsmouth in June 1776. That summer the Americans began fortifying Hospital Point, which earlier had been occupied by Dunmore. They built parapets fourteen feet high and fifteen feet thick. The defenders would be able to fire upon the enemy from forty-two embrasures. The structure was imposing enough to be formally denominated Fort Nelson. Before the fortifications were complete, the soldiers knew they were fighting for a new nation. Richard Henry Lee, a Tidewater Virginian sent to the Congress in Philadelphia, had introduced Virginia's resolution for independence. The resulting Declaration of Independence written by another Virginian, Thomas Jefferson, had been adopted by the Congress.

The first real test of Fort Nelson came in May 1779 when Commodore Sir George Collier anchored offshore with six warships and twenty-eight transports. Aboard the transports were eighteen hundred troops commanded by Brig. Gen. Edward Mathew. On the second day, May 9, the soldiers went ashore at the Portsmouth Parish Glebe (now the Port Norfolk section of Portsmouth) and attacked Fort Nelson from the rear. Despite its imposing redoubts on three sides, its rear was highly vulnerable. Apparently its planners had not anticipated an "end run" of the kind executed by the British. Hopelessly outnumbered, the American commander, Maj. Thomas Mathews, withdrew his company under cover of darkness. They gained a little time by leaving the flag flying. The British were surprised first when their shots were not returned as the new day dawned, and again a little later when they discovered the fort was vacant.

Collier easily occupied Portsmouth, Gosport, and Norfolk, and torched Suffolk. He boasted that in setting fires that "totally consumed" the Gosport Shipyard, operated by the Virginia Navy since Sprowle's flight, he had destroyed "the most considerable [shipyard] in America." He said, "This conflagration in the night appeared grand beyond description though the sight was a melancholy one." After burning or capturing 137 vessels in Hampton Roads and dismantling Fort Nelson, he sailed for New York, rejoicing that he had cut the main southern supply line to Washington's army and destroyed the principal shipbuilding center in Virginia.

All harbor traffic, whether of friend or foe, halted that winter when Hampton Roads froze over—an unusual occurrence.

A British fleet of sixty vessels, carrying five thousand troops commanded by Maj. Gen. Alexander Leslie, entered Hampton Roads in October 1780. Some were landed at Newport News and seized Hampton while others went ashore at Portsmouth. By November 3, between twenty-five hundred and three thousand of the invaders were concentrated in and around the town. With most of Virginia's soldiers and arms actively engaged in major theaters of war, Gov. Thomas Jefferson was unable to rescue Portsmouth. By mid-November Leslie was called away by Gen. Lord Cornwallis, who wished him to augment his lordship's great army then marching northward through the Carolinas.

Almost at year's end another British fleet entered

Hampton Roads bearing troops. After plundering along the James River and raiding Williamsburg and Richmond, they occupied Portsmouth. Their commander was the officer detested above all others by the Americans—Brig. Gen. Benedict Arnold who, after valiant service with the Continental Army, had turned traitor. Arnold made his headquarters in a private home apparently at the intersection of High and Crawford streets and converted a sugar warehouse at the south end of Crawford Street into a barracks and prison. He began construction of a crescent of fortifications embracing much of the town.

American plans to capture the traitor were frustrated by British naval power and the inability of the French fleets to effect a timely juncture with American troops. Arnold nevertheless was having his problems. Provisions were short, sickness plagued his forces, and he received little respect even from his fellow officers.

British Maj. Gen. William Phillips, bringing with him more than two thousand additional troops in March 1781, replaced Arnold as commander of British forces in the Portsmouth area. From their base in Portsmouth, the two British generals marched on Williamsburg and on Petersburg, where Phillips died. Arnold was therefore again in command when the British force in Southeastern Virginia rendezvoused with Cornwallis, who had marched from North Carolina.

After riding through a large area of Lower Tidewater in June and the first week of July, Cornwallis proceeded to Portsmouth with the idea of embarking for New York with his entire command. The earl's troops were actually boarding the ships when he received a message from his commander-in-chief, Sir Henry Clinton, instructing him to "take a post and hold it." Cornwallis considered remaining in Portsmouth but also toyed with the idea of going to Old Point. Finally, on August 20, he evacuated Portsmouth, ironically explaining to his superiors his conviction that by going to "a place called Yorktown," he could bring the war to a speedy conclusion. Of course Washington, with the aid of French Admiral de Grasse, was able to bottle up Cornwallis' army at Yorktown. On October 19, 1781, the earl's scarlet-coated troops marched out to the tune of "The World Turned Upside Down" to lay down their arms before Washington's threadbare legions. There is a persistent tradition that on that day the bell ringer for the Portsmouth Parish Church performed his duties so vigorously that he cracked the bell.

In the years following, Portsmouth delighted in honoring its Revolutionary heroes. Foremost among these was Richard Dale, first lieutenant to John Paul Jones and commander of the *Bonhomme Richard*'s gun deck and main battery in its historic victory over the *Serapis*. Dale, who had gone to sea at the age of thirteen or fourteen, later became commodore of the Mediterranean Squadron.

Capt. John Cox, another naval hero from Portsmouth, escaped British captivity to play a daring role in thrilling escapades in the Caribbean. He lived fifty-six years after the surrender at Yorktown to recount his adventures, dying in 1837 in his eighty-fifth year.

James Lafayette, a black man, who had spent a great deal of time in Portsmouth, had been one of the most important American spies in the Revolution. As a slave, he had not been suspected by the British when he gathered information during their occupation of the city. He reported to General Lafayette and developed such rapport with him that he later adopted the Marquis' surname. For his valuable services, the General Assembly of Virginia gave James Lafayette his freedom and an annual pension.

Some heroes, carried to Portsmouth or its vicinity by the tides of war, chose to remain after the end of hostilities. Col. Bernard Magnien, a Frenchman who came with General Lafayette to the aid of the Americans, lived on in Portsmouth, becoming a trustee of the town. His final resting place is in Trinity Churchyard not far from the grave of "Willis Wilson, Esquire, of the Town of Portsmouth, late Colonel, 4th Regiment Artillery...a patriot." Antonio S. Bilisoly, who served with de Grasse's fleet, settled in Portsmouth and died in the town in 1845 at the age of eighty-six. He is honored as the patriarch of one of Portsmouth's most prominent families. To Col. Josiah Parker, who settled in town after the war, Portsmouth citizens showed their appreciation by helping to send him to Congress as first representative from the new district.

■

James Lafayette, a slave who was one of America's most effective spies, operated in the Portsmouth area to supply information to the Marquis de Lafayette. So great was his admiration for the French general that he adopted his surname. In gratitude for his services, the General Assembly of Virginia freed him and voted him a pension for life.
Courtesy Valentine Museum, Richmond, Virginia

General Lord Cornwallis, whose decision to abandon Portsmouth led to his surrender at Yorktown.
Picture from James Thacher's Military Journal of the American Revolution, 1862

The stone house at the intersection of High and Crawford streets which served as Benedict Arnold's headquarters in Portsmouth was sketched by the celebrated historical artist Benson John Lossing on the late afternoon of December 24, 1849, working rapidly to take advantage of the fading light.
Sketch from Lossing's Field Book of the Revolution, 1859

Two monuments in Portsmouth honor Commodore Dale—a handsome bas relief (1) on Washington Street (lower right) and a rugged stone (2) at the site of his birth in Waterview. A portion of the home (3) at the birthplace (immediately above) apparently was built by Dale himself.
Ramona H. Mapp photos

Three monuments to Lafayette commemorate his association with Portsmouth: a pyramid in City Park (1) which once bore his profile, a plaque at the northwest corner of High and Crawford streets (2) where he watched a parade in his honor in 1824, and the Bicentennial Arch at Marquis de Lafayette Park (3) which recalls a temporary structure erected to welcome him to the city.
Photo of the arch taken by William J. Maloney; the other two by Ramona H. Mapp

3.

2.

1.

The USS Chesapeake, one of the most famous United States naval ships, was built in the Navy Yard at Gosport under the direction of Commodore Richard Dale.
Photo courtesy Portsmouth Naval Shipyard Museum

chapter five
PEACEFUL GROWTH

With the end of the Revolution, Portsmouth proceeded to repair the damages of the war and prepare the way for future growth. In 1783, the year that the Treaty of Paris officially ended hostilities, the citizens successfully petitioned the General Assembly of Virginia to empower the Town Trustees to levy an annual tax for public improvements and to regulate markets and remove nuisances. The Assembly also authorized the building of a town market-house, which was erected in the center of High Street between Crawford Street and the waterfront.

In 1784 other petitions to the General Assembly obtained for the town the right to annex Gosport and to subdivide lands adjacent to the shipyard for sale to individuals.

But there was still a highly visible barrier to Portsmouth progress, one that stirred patriotic ire. Though British vessels traded in United States ports as freely as before the Revolution, England's Navigation Acts barred American ships from the profitable West Indies trade. Merchants, mariners, and shipbuilders of the town in 1785 petitioned the Commonwealth of Virginia, asserting that if the situation were not "speedily redressed" it "must shortly end in a total loss of that valuable branch of mechanics, shipbuilding," and would destroy a "nursery for seamen, the great bulwark of maritime powers.... When we cast our eye over our harbors we see there scarcely a flag, but of that nation which so lately displayed theirs in these very harbors, with intentions the most hostile and diabolical, this too at a time when not a vessel belonging to the United States, even in distress, is permitted to enter any of the ports or harbors in the British West Indian Islands."

The condition was not soon remedied, and Portsmouth's growth was more sluggish than had been anticipated in the heady days following victory at Yorktown. The census of 1790 showed Portsmouth as the home of 1,712 persons: 1,039 whites, 616 slaves, and 47 free Negroes.

Still the town had its charms. Testimony of this comes not only from local boosters of the day but also from a far more objective source, the sophisticated French traveler Moreau de St. Mery. In 1794 he wrote that Portsmouth's "three hundred houses do not border the streets. They are so spaced that the impression is of wide and beautiful avenues." He admired the beauty of the lawns, but noted one detail that certainly would not please a modern chamber of commerce. He reported that grass grew even in the streets. He noted that wooden houses prevailed, as indeed they did in all Virginia communities of the day, but said that "a few extremely pretty ones are brick." Brick, too, were the market and the parish church (Trinity), which he admired as "neat and well kept." Nothing in Portsmouth impressed him more than the great vista of High Street, so wide as to seem an "open square" running the length of the town.

St. Mery was interested in two Gosport institutions, the shipyard and the distillery, but deplored the general lack of commerce in Portsmouth. "Its location," he said, "has some genuine advantages over that of Norfolk. The water is deeper at the wharves, and the drinking water is better than Norfolk's. It is better arranged, less hot and swampy, and therefore healthier."

The charm of Portsmouth women was strong

enough to overcome even the writer's Gallic prejudice against the English language. "The women in these places [Portsmouth and Norfolk] as elsewhere in Virginia, have the sweetest of voices; and this charm, perhaps one of the greatest the fair sex can possess, is so pronounced that the English language, ordinarily far from sweet, becomes something quite different on their seductive lips."

The very year in which St. Mery visited the town, 1794, saw international developments stimulating the industry whose lack he had bemoaned. Because of the war with the Barbary States, Congress authorized construction of six frigates—three of which, the *Constitution*, the *Constellation*, and the *Chesapeake*—were destined for great fame. One of these, *Chesapeake*, was built under the direction of Capt. (later Commodore) Richard Dale in the shipyard at Gosport. Though a declaration of peace in 1795 halted construction, a threat from France in 1798 brought its completion. In 1801 the federal government purchased the Gosport yard. Ever since then it has been a mainstay of a national navy and of Portsmouth's economy.

Already underway was a movement by enterprising Portsmouth citizens to have the courthouse for Norfolk County moved from Washington (later Berkley) to their town. The operations of a county court drew people from all over the jurisdiction, providing increased business for tavernkeepers and merchants. Erection of the courthouse at Washington in 1792 had not only enhanced the growth of existing businesses but had caused new ones to spring up. To entice Norfolk County citizens, a group of Portsmouth residents proposed to build, at their own expense, a new courthouse and prison "on the ground set apart for that purpose in the town of Portsmouth." Construction began in high hopes, but the promoters ran out of funds. Norfolk County, however, appropriated the sum required for that purpose and in May 1803 moved its seat of government to Portsmouth. The new courthouse and the prison—complete with stocks, whipping post, necessary house, well, and pump—stood respectively on the northeast and northwest corners of High and Court streets, locations traditionally designated for those purposes by the far-sighted founder, Colonel Crawford.

High Street was as wide when French tourist Moreau de St. Mery admired it in 1794 as today when it bears 1988 traffic. The visitor said its width gave it the look of an "open square" running the length of the town. This view is westward from the waterfront.
William J. Maloney photo

Norfolk County's seat of government was moved in 1803 to the intersection of Court and High streets and remained there until 1962. The building shown here is not the 1803 Court House but its 1846 successor as it appeared on a winter's day in the 1930s. To the right is the Portsmouth Municipal Building (now razed) erected in 1912.
Photo courtesy Portsmouth Public Library

Capt. James Lawrence, who, in his dying words aboard the USS Chesapeake, a vessel built in Portsmouth, gave the United States Navy its watchword: "Don't give up the ship."
Photo courtesy Portsmouth Naval Shipyard Museum

chapter six
BACK TO WAR

An international event intimately connected with Portsmouth dramatized in June 1807 an interruption to the commercial progress of the town and of the entire United States. Britain and France were at war and Britain was boarding American vessels to impress (draft into naval service) any of its own nationals found aboard. Just outside the three-mile limit off Hampton Roads, the British frigate *Leopard* hailed the U.S. frigate *Chesapeake*, commanded by Comm. James Barron, and demanded the right to search for British deserters. Upon Barron's refusal the *Leopard* opened fire, killing three of the crew, injuring eighteen, and seizing four whom they claimed as deserters. The American ship limped back into Hampton Roads. Outrage boiled in the United States, nowhere more than in Portsmouth. The *Chesapeake* was the first United States naval frigate built in the Gosport Shipyard. Its commander, Commodore Barron, was a Hampton Roads native with strong ties to Portsmouth.

President Jefferson ordered all British ships of war to leave United States territorial waters and demanded reparations for the *Leopard's* attack. In October the British stepped up the impressment program and insisted on the withdrawal of Jefferson's proclamation as a prerequisite to payment of indemnity. With negotiations at a stalemate, the president obtained from Congress an Embargo Act interdicting virtually all commerce with foreign nations. It remained in force from December 22, 1807, until March 15, 1809, and was superseded by the Non-Intercourse Act which forbade trade specifically with France and Great Britain. Idle ships rode at anchor in Hampton Roads or made for freshwater anchorages. Warehouses were locked.

Shipbuilders and mercantile workers were unemployed. Continued incidents between Great Britain and the United States led in 1812 to war between the two countries. The armed forces of the United States were small, but this disadvantage was offset by Britain's long-drawn supply lines and by the drain of her simultaneous struggle with Napoleon. As a seaport community, the site of an important naval shipyard, on the great harbor commanding the water routes to the nation's capital, Portsmouth was a prime target and a highly vulnerable one. Anxiety mounted in February 1812 when a British squadron under Adm. Sir John B. Warren blockaded the harbor.

A motley collection of armed American vessels stretching in an arc between Craney Island and Lambert's Point stood defensively between Portsmouth and the potential invader. Craney Island, on Portsmouth's doorstep, was guarded by state militia, some regulars, and some seamen from the *Constellation*—in all about 750 men. On June 22 the defenders were attacked by about 1,500 seamen and marines and about 2,600 troops under Brig. Gen. Sir Sidney Beckwith. As the British approached aboard a fleet of fifty barges, the vastly outnumbered Americans knew that their enemies' ultimate goal was destruction of the town of Portsmouth and its shipyard. But the British never got past Craney Island. The heroism of the defenders and their deadly artillery fire turned back the would-be invaders. Conspicuous in the American defense was Grimes Battery, Portsmouth's own unit, under the command of Capt. Arthur Emmerson. Before the War of 1812 came to an end in 1815, the British had repeatedly attacked Chesapeake Bay communities and had even captured and burned Washington, D. C., but they never again attacked Portsmouth or any other place in South Hampton Roads.

One distant battle of the war, on June 1, 1813, had special poignancy for Portsmouth. With more gallantry than prudence, Capt. James Lawrence, commanding the *Chesapeake* off the coast of Massachusetts, had accepted a challenge from British Capt. P. B. V. Broke of the *Shannon*. The American ship was raked with fire from stem to stern, disabled, and captured. But Captain Lawrence's dying words were reported as "Don't give up the ship." Despite the American defeat, that last order became "the rallying cry of the United States Navy." Portsmouth people were moved by the heroic demise of the Portsmouth-built vessel that had played so important a role in the succession of hostilities leading to war.

■

Commodore Barron's tomb (inside iron enclosure in foreground) is in the Trinity Episcopal Churchyard. Elsewhere in the cemetery are the tombs of such Revolutionary patriots as Col. Bernard Magnien and Col. Willis Wilson. In the left is the rear of Trinity Church (built 1762, enlarged 1829, remodeled 1893) with its bell tower rising in the background. Across the street is the old Town Hall with the Town Clock in its cupola. J. C. Emmerson photo, courtesy Portsmouth Public Library

Commodore James Barron, who commanded the USS Chesapeake in its encounter with the HMS Leopard in 1807. A result of the quarrel growing out of the incident was Barron's famous duel in 1820 with Commodore Stephen Decatur. Photo courtesy Portsmouth Naval Shipyard Museum

portsmouth schools

Students of the Glasgow Street Academy poured out into the schoolyard, onto the sidewalks, and into the street one day in 1885 to have their picture taken. It was a proud day for the school, and its principal, L. P. Slater, stood tall on the curb near the tree. That year the institution graduated the first public high school class in the history of Portsmouth. Though operating as a public school since 1847, it had begun as a private one. Incorporated in 1825 as the Portsmouth Academy, with a Reverend Mr. Freeman as headmaster, it had as trustees some of the most prominent men in the area: Holt Wilson, Thurmer Hoggard, Swepson Whitehead, Joseph Schoolfield, Beverly Bayton, John Hodges, Richard Carney, and William Wright.

In 1839 it was transformed into the Virginia Literary, Scientific, and Military Academy with Capt. Alden Partridge, formerly acting superintendent of the United States Military Academy at West Point, as headmaster. The building, on Glasgow Street between Middle and Crawford, was used as a hospital in the yellow fever epidemic of 1855 and afterwards as an orphanage for several hundred children who had lost their parents in the epidemic. For a while it was a yeast powder factory. During the Civil War it was a barracks for the Confederates and then for the victorious Federals before returning to its original function. Photo courtesy Portsmouth Public Library

Another Portsmouth Academy, unconnected with the earlier one, was established in 1868 by W. H. (Cap'n Billy) Stokes. In this 1901 photo, Mr. Stokes (the grandfather of Dr. Ralph M. Stokes, Jr.) sits in a wheelchair in the doorway at 401 Crawford Street. His sister, Miss Emma, a teacher in the school, stands at his side. The building was destroyed to make way for the new federal building completed in 1961.
Photo from the Emmerson Collection, courtesy Portsmouth Public Library

One school, within the boundaries of Portsmouth since 1968, is much older than either of those known as Portsmouth Academy—indeed, in its antecedents, it is one of the oldest public schools in Virginia. Churchland Academy, whose last home was condemned to destruction in 1988, was established as the Craney Island School, a public institution. It was rebuilt in 1840 and its name was changed to Sycamore Hill School. In 1854 it received a bequest of fifteen hundred dollars—then a considerable sum—from James H. Carney, a Churchland planter who freed his slaves and contributed generously to schools in Virginia and North Carolina. Carney provided that his gift to the local institution be invested and the proceeds used "to provide free education for all the children of the community" and for no other purpose. The school was greatly enlarged and one branch, to be known as Churchland Academy, was "incorporated for instruction in higher English and the classics."
Ira Richardson photo

Superintendents

Only nine people have served as Superintendent in the 140 years of the Portsmouth Public School system.

The first Superintendent of Schools and organizer of the system was Rev. Thomas Hume, who served from 1848 to about 1860. There was no public high school, and there were two broad divisions—primary and elementary. Portsmouth people were impressed with the fact that he paid his own expenses to attend the National Teachers' meeting in Philadelphia in 1850. He organized the first teachers' association in Virginia and possibly in the entire South. Dr. Hume was simultaneously pastor of Court Street Baptist Church and added eight hundred members during his ministry. His dual capacity presented no problems of sectarianism or of conflict between church and state. A contemporary account, reprinted in the Portsmouth Star on June 5, 1901, said: "Among the people of all religions and no religions he was esteemed and venerated." The same source praised his "smooth and tender eloquence."

Mr. Hume remained in the city throughout the yellow fever epidemic of 1855, helping the sick, comforting the bereaved, and taking care of numerous orphans. After his death, one resident of the area wrote: "To his fatherly care many are indebted for the positions which they now occupy." He was a man of great versatility and prodigious energy. Besides serving education both as superintendent of schools and treasurer of the corporation of Chesapeake Female College, and religion both as pastor of Court Street Baptist Church and president of the Baptist General Association of Virginia, he was president of the Portsmouth Insurance Company, and a director of the Bank of Portsmouth and of the Seaboard and Roanoke Railroad.
Photo courtesy Portsmouth Public Schools

Maj. James Francis Crocker was superintendent from 1871 to 1882. In 1872 the system consisted of Glasgow Street Male School, Glasgow Street Female School, Newtown Academy, and a fourth school attended by both male and female blacks but in sexually segregated classes. At the Newtown Academy, under Major Crocker's administration, boys and girls attended the same classes for the first time in Portsmouth.
Photo courtesy Portsmouth Public Schools

While Major Crocker was superintendent, the Chestnut Street School, Portsmouth's first school erected expressly as a school for blacks, was built in 1879 at the intersection of South and Chestnut streets. It was the ancestor of I. C. Norcom High School.
Photo courtesy Portsmouth Public Library

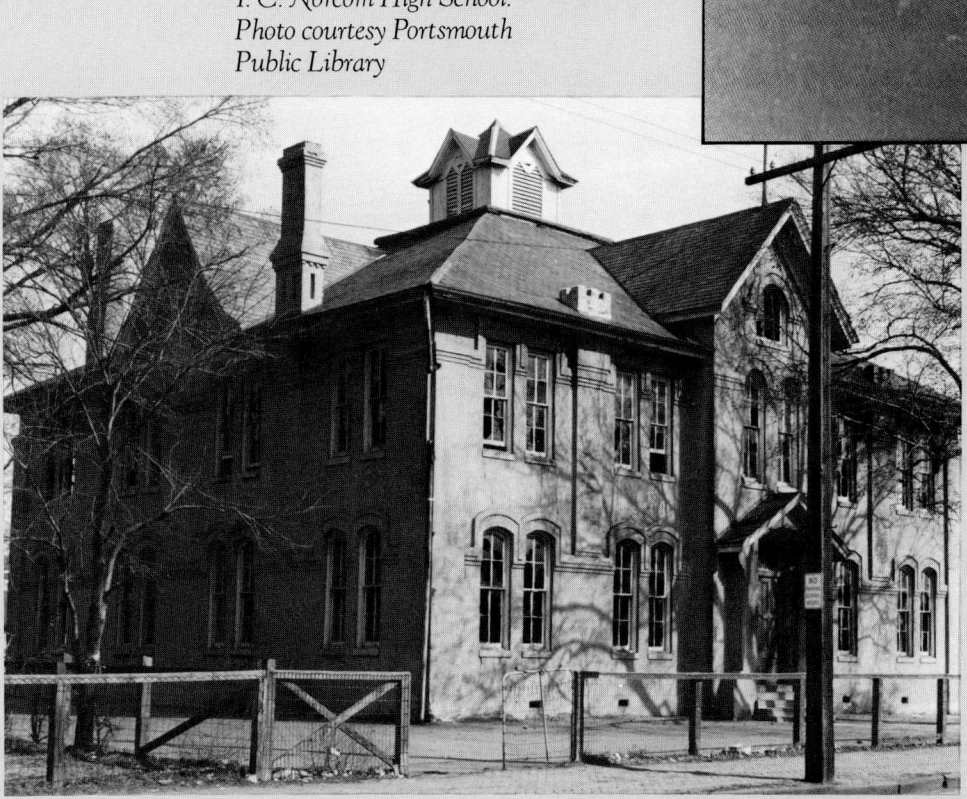

Maj. Griffin F. Edwards, who was Superintendent from 1882 to 1886, purchased land at the intersection of Green and Columbia streets for erection in 1886 of a building housing elementary and high schools. Subjects in the elementary curriculum were language, arithmetic, reading, spelling, writing, geography, and hygiene. High school subjects were English, Latin, physics, algebra, and arithmetic. Portsmouth's first public high school graduation, at the Glasgow Street Academy, was in 1885.
Photo courtesy Portsmouth Public Schools

The Green Street School, built in 1886 and used at first for both elementary and high school students, was used as a high school as late as 1908. It still presented a neat appearance when this photo was made on June 8, 1958 (1). Elementary school children occupied this classroom, possibly in the 1940s (2).
Photos courtesy Portsmouth Public Library

John C. Ashton, superintendent from 1886 to 1909, built two schools. A much admired structure, known as the Fifth Ward School, was erected at Cooke and North streets in 1897. Its name was later changed to Cooke Street School and still later to John Marshall (2). In 1908 property at the intersection of King and Washington streets was acquired for the erection of Portsmouth High School. Though Mr. Ashton had retired before the school opened in September 1909, he was still superintendent when the cornerstone was laid the preceding January 4. Photos courtesy Portsmouth Public Schools

Harry A. Hunt was superintendent from 1909 to 1950. Neither date is a misprint; when Mr. Hunt retired after forty-one years in office, he had been a division superintendent of schools longer than anyone else alive in Virginia, possibly than anybody else in Virginia history. For generations of Portsmouth students the lean man with the rimless spectacles was as much a symbol of the schools as Uncle Sam was of the United States. His face was stern in repose, but on being greeted by a friend or friendly child, literally flushed with delight as he broke into a winning smile. As an elderly man he seemed equally proud of his skill at golf and at lightning-swift mathematical calculations. This superbly disciplined man surprised people when he told them that at the age of six, unbeknown to his straitlaced family, he had become a secret drinker, carrying a tiny flask in his hip pocket. A sermon he heard at the age of eight, delivered by a minister unaware of its applicability to so young an auditor, convinced Harry Hunt of the evils of alcohol and he foreswore it for the rest of his life. The city's population grew from about 33,000 to 50,745 during Mr. Hunt's tenure and his responsibilities increased tremendously. A formidable logician, he defended the schools' prerogatives with unyielding consistency. Harry A. Hunt Junior High School was named in his honor.
Photo courtesy Portsmouth Public Schools

J. Leon Codd, after teaching in the Prentis Park and Cooke Street schools, became principal of Portsmouth High School in 1907. The school became Woodrow Wilson High School in 1919, and Mr. Codd remained as principal until 1941. A blast from his whistle, which he carried like a badge of office, struck terror to students in the halls when they belonged in class. Behind the sometimes severe exterior was a kindly, witty, and highly intelligent man whom the youngsters deeply respected even when they called him Jake behind his back. Mr. Codd was elected to the House of Delegates from Portsmouth in 1946 and 1948.
Photo courtesy Woodrow Wilson High School

Portsmouth High school, built in 1908, was on the east side of Washington Street between High and King streets. It was later renamed Briggs School in honor of Frank Briggs, a longtime member of the School Board. The building, seen here in 1920, was being used for some School Board offices when it burned in 1960.
Photo courtesy Portsmouth Public Library

With young women in middie blouses and young men in dark suits, backed by the Virginia flag and a forty-eight-star United States flag, the graduating class of Portsmouth High School presented a dignified appearance in 1914. Fifth from the right in the rear, with his head over part of the Seal of Virginia, is Principal J. Leon Codd.
Photo courtesy Portsmouth Public Library

This one of two buildings composing the Port Norfolk Elementary School (annexed in 1919) housed the principal's office and was the nerve center of the institution. A feature of the building that proved irresistible to many pupils was a spiral fire escape in the rear. The edge of the adjacent school building shows on the far right. The school had its own museum and newspaper, and in the 1930s was one of the few elementary schools in the South using sophisticated audio-visual aids.
Photo courtesy Portsmouth Public Library

Pinners Point Elementary School (annexed in 1919) rose abruptly from its level yard in the 1940s. Today its site is covered by the Portsmouth Marine Terminal.
Photo courtesy Portsmouth Public Library

The cornerstone for Portsmouth's first Woodrow Wilson High School (now Harry Hunt Junior High School) is laid on May 18, 1917, in the 1800 block of High Street.
Photo courtesy Portsmouth Public Library

Masonic officer William Trafton (in apron) officiates at cornerstone laying for the new Woodrow Wilson High School in 1953.
Photo courtesy Portsmouth Public Library

Portsmouth's first Woodrow Wilson High School was contained within this building until the addition of a second building to house a new gymnasium and the physical education department.
Photo courtesy Portsmouth Public Library

Alf J. Mapp, Sr., was superintendent of schools from 1950 to 1965. He built a new I. C. Norcom High School, a new Woodrow Wilson High School, and five new elementary schools. In 1960 the Portsmouth system acquired nine other schools by annexation. Mr. Mapp more than doubled teachers' salaries. He pressed for improvement of reading skills, and in 1959 received, on behalf of Portsmouth Public Schools, the Betts Reading Clinic Award (first place, United States and Canada) "in recognition of outstanding service and achievement in the improvement of reading." In 1961 he became the thirty-eighth United States educator to be named "Leader in Education." The Portsmouth Public Schools were slected by the United States Office of Education as one of three model systems for national study and emulation. Peaceful integration of the schools began in his administration. Alf J. Mapp Junior High School was named in his honor.

In 1968 an oil portrait of Mr. Mapp was placed in the library of the College of William and Mary and a plaque dedicated to him was placed in Phi Beta Kappa Hall. The inscription, in part, reads: "As an undergraduate, he won formal recognition for literary, forensic, athletic and leadership activities, receiving a number and variety of honors unexcelled in the history of the college. Following World War II he was instrumental in the organization of the St. Helena Division of the College of William and Mary. His forty-seven years as a school administrator in Virginia were climaxed by service as superintendent of Portsmouth Public Schools from 1950 to 1965. He pioneered in audio-visual education in the elementary schools of the Commonwealth. He won national acclaim as a school administrator and international recognition for his achievements in the improvement of reading skills."

Photo courtesy Portsmouth Public Schools

Dr. M. E. Alford, superintendent from 1965 to 1984, had the task of fully implementing the 1971 court order integrating the schools. The process went forward peacefully. As population concentrations shifted, the Alford administration closed five schools and opened eight. The superintendent planned and developed special centers for handicapped students and converted I. C. Norcom High School into a "Comprehensive Technical Center" preparing students both for technical occupations and for entrance into higher education programs in technology. Dr. Alford's previous experience as president of Frederick College (now Tidewater Community College) was helpful to him in assessing the high schools' role in preparing college-bound students. A musical theater program, said to be the first of its kind in the nation, was instituted in the Alford years. Dr. Alford's persuasive skills were always manifest when he presented the School Board's budget to City Council.
Photo courtesy Portsmouth
Public Schools

*The new Norcom High School, whose cornerstone was laid in 1953, won a blue ribbon at a national architectural exhibition. At first predominantly black, the school later was integrated along with the rest of the Portsmouth system.
Photo courtesy Norcom High School*

*Grandchildren of I. C. Norcom are photographed in 1953 at the dedication of the high school named for him. The woman second from right is unidentified. Others are (left to right) James G. Norcom, Jr.; Lt. Col. Henry Charles Norcom; Mrs. Mary Norcom Majette; and Mrs. Rachel Norcom Smith. I. C. Norcom, a graduate of Andover Academy and Yale University, was the first black principal in Portsmouth Public Schools. His son, James G. Norcom, taught forty-one years in Portsmouth, and James G., Jr. taught thirty-three.
Photo courtesy Portsmouth
Public Library*

*The two buildings of the old Norcom High School became respectively (left to right) Peabody Elementary School and Riddick-Weaver Elementary School.
Photo courtesy Portsmouth
Public Library*

The old Cradock High and Elementary School Building, shown here in the 1920s, was replaced by the new Alf J. Mapp Junior High School in 1965. Photo courtesy Portsmouth Public Library

*An anchor, symbol of the Cradock Admirals, stands at the main entrance to Cradock High School on George Washington Highway. Seen in this perspective, it has the look of abstract sculpture. Like the neighborhood in which it is located, the school bears the name of British Rear Admiral Sir Christopher Cradock. Principal streets in the area are named for heroes of the sea.
Ramona H. Mapp photo*

May Day used to be celebrated with dancing around a Maypole and participation in athletic contests, as in this 1952 photo of the observance at Ann Street School.
Photo courtesy Allen M. Eckstine

Miss Clyde White, English and journalism teacher at Wilson High School who trained many professional writers, looks over proof pages of The Student, *national award-winning student newspaper.*
Photo courtesy Portsmouth Public Library

Students and teachers move about outside the new Woodrow Wilson High School. Doors on the right lead to the T. A. Willet Auditorium, which serves also as Portsmouth's principal civic auditorium. At the time of its dedication it was said that it could "handle a production of Aida, including the elephants." Ballet companies said that its stage was the best for their art between Washington and Atlanta. A refurbishing of the auditorium was completed in 1988.
Undated photo courtesy Portsmouth Public Library

Miss Virginia Girffith, beloved Latin teacher of Woodrow Wilson High School, stands by the bust of an old friend, Julius Caesar. The record of war stamps sales on the chalk board indicates that the photo was made during World War II. For many years Miss Griffith took a course at the University of Virginia virtually every summer for intellectual refreshment. Her classical interests were excited in childhood when she wondered why her father's horse was named Bucephalus.
Photo courtesy Portsmouth Public Library

Ann Street pupils and alumni were proud of the handsome Corinthian-columned facade of this school.
Photo courtesy Portsmouth Public Library

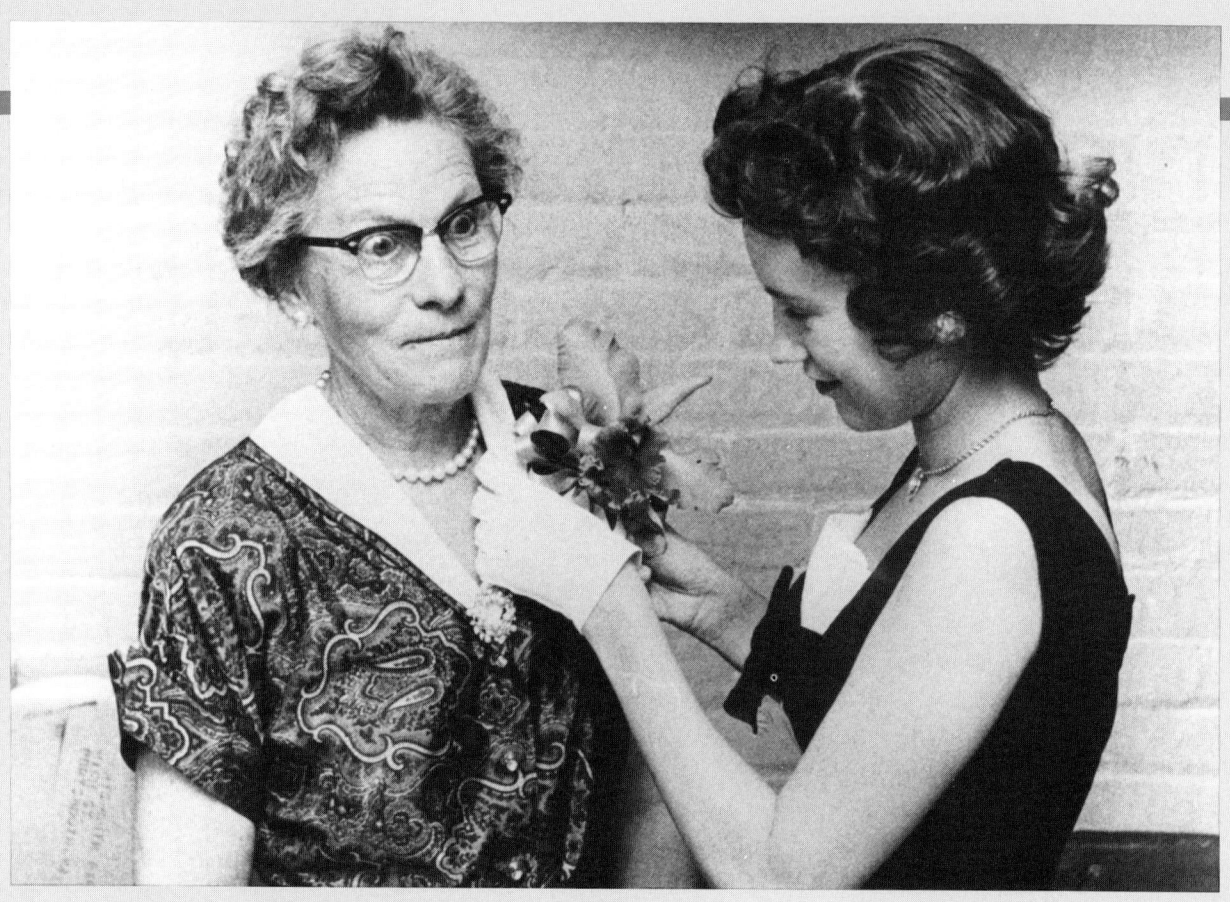

Miss Florence Hall, long-time assistant principal at Cooke Street School, receives a corsage at the start of her retirement party in June 1957. She is remembered for her kindness to children, her skill in training new principals, and her practice of climbing a twenty-foot upright ladder into the tower to ring a huge school bell by which people all over Park View set their watches. The bell today is in the riverside backyard of Raymond Wimbrough in Park Manor. The sight of it stirs in him fond memories of his school days and Miss Hall.
Photo of Miss Hall courtesy Allen M. Eckstine; the bell a Ramona H. Mapp photo

Anne Street and Cooke Street (John Marshall) schools were combined in the new Park View Elementary School, dedicated December 10, 1957. Here Principal Allen M. Eckstine points out a dedication exhibit to his predecessor, Kenneth A. Agee; School Board Chairwoman Emily N. Spong; former Superintendent of Schools Harry A. Hunt, and incumbent Superintendent Alf J. Mapp. Eckstine later was an assistant superintendent. Mrs. Spong, the first woman to be First Citizen of Portsmouth, was well known throughout Virginia for services to elementary, preparatory, and higher education. Photo courtesy Allen M. Eckstine

Built in 1897 as the Fifth Ward School, renamed Cooke Street and then John Marshall, this building functioned as a school until 1957.
Photo courtesy Portsmouth Public Library

The Portsmouth High School Girls Basketball Team presents a demure front in 1918.
Photo courtesy Portsmouth Public Library

Truxton Elementary School was erected to meet the needs of pupils in one of two planned communities designed to house the influx of Navy Yard workers in World War I.
Photo courtesy Portsmouth Public Library

At Norcom Commencement, mid-term 1956, are (left to right) Assistant Principal A. T. Edwards, Mrs. Ruth Waters, Mrs. Clarine Baltrip Waters, Rice Roberts, and Principal W. E. Waters. Mr. Waters bore a strong family resemblance to his cousin, actress and singer Ethel Waters. He is credited with helping to ease the city's passage from segregation to integration and with instilling high ideals of personal conduct in many young people. Waters Junior High School is named for him.
Photo courtesy Portsmouth Public Library

Principal Vernon Orton stands at a doorway of Clarke Junior High school. His widow, Audrey Orton, is a prominent civic leader and his son, Wayne, is now an assistant city manager.
Photo from the Rodgers Collection, courtesy Portsmouth Public Library

A Norcom High School homecoming parade marches down High Street on October 25, 1962. Unfortunately not visible here is the perennially most popular unit in all such processions, the Norcom High School Band. It won national honors, marched in gubernatorial inaugural parades and one presidential inaugural parade, and on trips was praised for its discipline off the field as well as on.
Photo courtesy Portsmouth Public Library

Clarke Junior High School dedication on April 27, 1958, brings together Vivian Watts, Superintendent Alf J. Mapp, Dr. A. G. Macklin, Dr. Macklin's daughter, and Supervisor Rufae J. Holmes. The school was named for S. J. Clarke, a deceased black principal.
Photo courtesy Portsmouth Public Library

Churchland High School looks serene on a day in 1988. The students call themselves "The Truckers," a reminder of the days near the turn of the century and afterwards when truck farming with shipments to Washington, Baltimore, New York, and Boston made Churchland one of the richest agricultural communities in the United States and for a while one of the richest in the world.
Ramona H. Mapp photo

Norcom High School students, on December 1, 1966, mail fruitcakes to alumni in the armed services.
Photo courtesy Portsmouth Public Library

Professor A. J. Lancaster (second from left), 'Prof' to his students, poses with the 1955 Woodrow Wilson High School Sextette and their accompanist, Dick Barnes. Each year Mr. Lancaster brought forth a new sextette to perform not only at school functions but also before civic clubs in Portsmouth and neighboring communities. The singers' faces changed through the years but the professor's remained ageless. He attributed his extraordinary energy to a vegetarian diet and a quart of orange juice a day. Mr. Lancaster came from England where he had been a precocious organist. Besides supervising music in the public schools, he was organist and choir director for Monumental Methodist Church, and long the leading spirit in the Portsmouth Community Concert Series, today the longest continuous series of the sort in Virginia. Once when a visitor asked to see Mr. Musick, a respected administrator in the school system, he was directed to Mr. Lancaster, who was indeed Portsmouth's Mr. Music.

Dick Barnes, after college and work with the late Fred Waring, became a music teacher in the Portsmouth Public Schools and organist and choir director at Monumental. Today he heads the music department on the Portsmouth campus of Tidewater Community College. The young vocalists in this picture, wearing the lace-edged collars, bobby socks, and soiled saddle oxfords popular at the time, are (left to right) Mary Frances Wiggins, Reba McIntyre, Nancy Eppling, Ruth Snowden, Catherine Williams, and Marjorie Sweeny.
Photo courtesy Dick Barnes

Wilson High School debating teams of 1937 were composed of (left to right, standing) Martha McGavock, Zelma Goodman, Shirley Schlitz, Mary Tom Bunting, and Jean Robison; (kneeling) Joseph Averitt, Warrington Sharp, Billy Spong, and Roy Smith. Martha McGavock, daughter of a popular elementary school principal, returned to Wilson as a teacher. Zelma Goodman, with her husband, Bernard Rivin, became co-owner of The Famous. Mary Tom Bunting became one of the city's pioneer female physicians. Billy Spong (W. B. Spong, Jr.) became a United States senator and dean of the law school at William and Mary.
Photo courtesy Portsmouth Public Library

St. Paul's Catholic Boys' School, operated by the Xazarian Brothers and often called "the Brothers' School," stood from 1891 to 1931 on the east side of Washington Street at the intersection with London Boulevard, not far from St. Paul's Catholic Church. Its predecessor, St. Joseph's Academy, was at Dinwiddie and King streets, 1876 to 1891.
Photo courtesy Portsmouth Public Library

*Miss Ora Churchill (1885-), a representative of one of Portsmouth's most prominent black families, was also one of the city's most beloved teachers, serving 1915-1966. Both professionally and as a civic leader, she worked to build bridges between blacks and whites and made both groups conscious of their common heritage.
Photo from the Rodgers Collection, courtesy Portsmouth Public Library*

*Philip Belton, here a school principal but later an assistant superintendent, awards adult education diplomas, probably in the early 1970s. Mr. Belton was a vice-chairman of the Portsmouth Revolutionary Bicentennial Committee and a highly esteemed civic leader.
Photo courtesy Portsmouth Public Library*

Dr. Rondle E. Edwards, superintendent from 1984 to 1987, was Portsmouth's first black superintendent of schools. He instituted a Public Information Office and a newsletter, Windows on Education. Dr. Edwards said that the keys to his efforts to improve the schools were "Mastery Learning" and "Reality Therapy."
Photo courtesy Portsmouth Public Schools

Dr. T. Mack Cherry became superintendent of schools in 1987. In the short while that he has been in office, Dr. Cherry has implemented a Family Life Education program, planned a new Churchland High School, and concentrated on building community relations.
Photo courtesy Portsmouth Public Schools

The Shea Terrace Elementary School, built in 1925, is shown here in the 1940s. Photo courtesy Portsmouth Public Library

Mrs. Margaret Bond (central figure), for many years chief librarian of I. C. Norcom High School, served also on the Portsmouth Public Library Board. Photo courtesy Lee F. Rogers Collection, Portsmouth Public Library

The main entrance of Tidewater Community College's Portsmouth Campus has been the gate of opportunity for many residents of Portsmouth and Suffolk. Originally Frederick College, a four-year liberal arts institution which opened September 12, 1961, it became Tidewater Community College in 1968 when its founder, Portsmouth philanthropist Frederick W. Beazley, donated the 750-acre campus and a million dollars to the Commonwealth of Virginia. In July 1987 the institution's name was changed to Frederick W. Beasley Portsmouth Campus of Tidewater Community College. The campus affords sweeping views of the James River and of the crossing now under construction between Suffolk and Newport News. Other TCC branches are in Chesapeake and Virginia Beach. Mr. Beazley, a self-made Atlantic Coast titan of the coal and ice industries, also founded Frederick Military Academy (now closed) in Portsmouth. The Frederick W. Beazley Foundation continues to be one of Portsmouth's principal philanthropic resources, particularly for the young and underprivileged.

Campus photo courtesy Tidewater Community College; Beazley photo courtesy Portsmouth Public Library

Col. Donald Woodard, commandant of Frederick Military Academy, awards Best Drilled Company honors to Company A. Founded by philanthropist Fred Beazley, the Portsmouth school operated from 1956 to 1985.
Photo courtesy Rufus Outland

The seventy-four gun USS Delaware enters a dock at the Navy Yard on June 17, 1833, in "the first drydocking in America." This drydock is still in use. Photo courtesy Portsmouth Public Library

chapter seven
RAPID PROGRESS

Portsmouth recovered quickly from the effects of the war and the embargo which preceded it. In the first year of peace, its citizens saw their first steamboat when a sidewheeler, the *Washington*, entered the Elizabeth River. The transition from sail to steam would be slow, but the small vessel was a harbinger. And meanwhile there was a tremendous increase in sail traffic. Between 1825 and 1830, the town was home to fifty-five sea captains engaged in international trade.

Enterprising citizens created a depository for their growing wealth. In 1827 they founded the Portsmouth Savings Society, generally considered the first bank in either Portsmouth or Norfolk.

Cultural growth quickened too. The Portsmouth Academy was incorporated in 1825 by leading citizens. In 1839, reflecting a more ambitious scope, it was renamed the Virginia Literary, Scientific, and Military Academy. Capt. Alden Partridge, formerly acting superintendent of the United States Military Academy at West Point, was engaged as headmaster. When Portsmouth and Norfolk County jointly formed a free school system, the same building in 1847 housed the town's first public school.

The Navy's first permanent hospital, to this day a handsome monument of Greek Revival architecture, opened its doors in 1830. In the same year, the town outgrew its dependence on the shipyard for fire protection and organized its own fire company.

Two years later, the area's first steam ferry, the *Gosport*, was placed in service. And in 1833, a stone drydock, today the oldest still in use in the United States, was opened at the Gosport yard. Its reception of the *Delaware* was excitedly hailed as the first drydocking in America.

But the town was becoming increasingly interested in another form of transportation. In 1832 it became one of the first American communities to organize a railroad, the Portsmouth and Roanoke Railroad Company. The presidency of Capt. Arthur Emmerson and the employment of Col. Claude Crozet, an internationally distinguished engineer, insured respect. Its first engine ran from Portsmouth to Suffolk in 1834. Later it would grow into the famous Seaboard Air Line Railroad, with corporate headquarters in Portsmouth.

Civic pride soared in 1837 when the town got its first brick sidewalks, cobbled gutters, and flagstone curbs and crossings. An attractive community greeted the increasing numbers who came on business. By 1835 they could stay in Portsmouth's first hotel, the Crawford House. Two other hotels, the Ocean House and the Macon House, were started in 1853. The next year the opening of a bathing beach at the north end of Court Street was an added attraction.

The roster of visitors between 1824 and 1859 is an indication of the town's growing importance. The list includes the Marquis de Lafayette, Chief Black Hawk, Gen. Winfield Scott, Daniel Webster, and Presidents Andrew Jackson, Martin Van Buren, John Tyler, James K. Polk, Millard Fillmore, and James Buchanan.

Portsmouth citizens could read the story of progress and the accounts of visiting dignitaries in their own newspapers, beginning in 1827 with the *Virginia Palladium and Portsmouth Commercial Advertiser* and including within eleven years the *Portsmouth Republican and Virginia*

Commercial Gazette, the *Portsmouth Advocate*, the *Times and Commercial Advertiser* and the *Old Dominion*.

News in 1846 was both exciting and disturbing. On May 13, the Congress of the United States declared war on Mexico. The nation went to war in a divided state of mind, the majority arguing that United States honor and security demanded that Mexico be struck a punishing blow while a sizeable minority argued that the United States was planning an unjust invasion. Opposition centered in the North. Virginia, like most of the South, supported the administration in Washington. Company F, First Regiment, Virginia Foot—Portsmouth's own, commanded by Captain John P. Young—left for Mexico.

A more lasting monument of Portsmouth's activities in 1846 is the courthouse which was dedicated on July 20. Instead of repairing the 1803 courthouse on the northeast corner of High and Court streets, the justices of Norfolk County decided to replace it with a new one on the northwest corner. The General Assembly of Virginia authorized the move with the proviso that, if the town should become a city, it would be permitted to share the building equally with the county. The architect was William B. Singleton, Portsmouth native practicing his profession with conspicuous success in St. Louis. The new building was an imposing one with a handsome cupola. The courtroom measured fifty-seven by fifty-four feet and there were spacious offices, including that of the county clerk. Today this building houses a children's museum and an art gallery, parts of the city's museum complex.

Portsmouth Naval Hospital (right in the large picture above) opened its doors in 1830 at the site of old Fort Nelson. The building was from the first an impressive example of Greek Revival architecture but a fifth floor and the familiar Jeffersonian dome were not added until 1907-09. Addition of the crowning feature was dictated by the practical need for more light in the operating room. Ships in the background reflect the gradual transition from sail to steam. In the small picture at lower right are the buildings of Portsmouth's Gosport Navy Yard.
Photo from a drawing on stone by F. Sachese, 1851; courtesy Portsmouth Public Library

Neo-classic facade of the Naval Hospital appears in photograph of a later date.
Photo courtesy Portsmouth Public Library

The Ocean House, a four-story hotel with a handsome grillework balcony, was built on the northeast corner of High and Court streets in 1853-1855 by Col. Winchester Watts and Col. Arthur Emmerson.
Photo courtesy Portsmouth Public Library

A courthouse designed by William B. Singleton, a Portsmouth native with a national reputation, was dedicated in 1846, the same year that some Portsmouth citizens marched off to service in the Mexican War.
Photo from Rolin and Keily's 1851 map of Portsmouth

the navy yard

The story of the Navy Yard has been a consistently reappearing thread in the weaving of Portsmouth history. Our narrative has sketched the Yard's beginning with Andrew Sprowle, its role in the Revolution and in the building of the new nation's Navy. It has told again of the international history made in the Civil War by the CSS *Virginia* (formerly the USS *Merrimac*), a product of the Portsmouth facility. Accounts of such famous Portsmouth-built ships as the *Chesapeake* and the USS *Langley*, the nation's first aircraft carrier, have been given; and attention has been directed to the role of the Yard in almost every war in which the United States has participated. But there are other, less celebrated facts about the Yard that deserve attention—some because they are associated with great events, some simply because they round out the personality of our community.

Here, as elsewhere in this book, the Norfolk Naval Shipyard, Portsmouth, Virginia, will not be referred to by that cumbersome and misleading title. The name Norfolk Navy Yard was given to the facility in 1862 when the federal government, occupying the conquered city of Portsmouth, did not find it necessary to poll the sentiments of its citizens. The name Norfolk was considered more meaningful than Gosport, and the name Portsmouth supposedly was precluded by a Portsmouth Navy Yard named for Portsmouth, New Hampshire. The whole business was complicated by the fact that the Norfolk Navy Yard was in Portsmouth and the Portsmouth Navy Yard was in Kittery, Maine. The change of the name of the Portsmouth, Virginia Yard to Norfolk Naval Shipyard, Portsmouth, Virginia, has not made the nomenclature more acceptable to Portsmouth people, even the most fiercely loyal employees of the Yard. Efforts to change the name to Portsmouth Naval Shipyard have so far proved futile, so our citizens continue to refer to the nation's greatest naval shipyard as the Navy Yard, Portsmouth's Navy Yard, the Navy Yard at Portsmouth, the Shipyard (in the way that some University of Virginia alumni refer to "*the* University") or simply the Yard. In this book, we do the same.

The USS Plymouth, *equipped with both steam engines and sails, dominates this picture from the mid 1870s. In the background are the frigate* St. Lawrence *(left) and the USS* Canadaigua *(right). Photo courtesy Portsmouth Public Library*

Three-masted sailing vessels and armored ships reminiscent of the Monitor vie for attention in this view of the Navy Yard a decade after the Civil War.
George May photo courtesy Portsmouth Public Library

Many Portsmouth residents can remember when visiting the Navy Yard was the most important part of the annual observance of Navy Day. Visitors board the submarine Adder in this circa 1906 photo.
Photo courtesy Portsmouth Public Library

Not nearly as famous as it deserves to be is the Yard's launching in 1892 of the USS Texas, first battleship built in the United States. Great timbers supporting the Texas, poised in drydock, seem like matchsticks. Officers and crew of the Texas, Captain W. T. Swinburne commanding, proudly pose. One young tar, hand on hip, leans out from his elevated perch (left of center) with the flair of a sailor in HMS Pinafore.

The carrier Lexington *sends a greeting to Portsmouth as tugs assist its progress toward the Navy Yard. People on Portsmouth's Seawall often have a grandstand view of some of the greatest ships in the United States Navy. Photo from the Rodgers Collection, courtesty Portsmouth Public Library*

The crew relaxes on the deck of the USS Monitor, the "cheese box on a raft." Photo courtesy Portsmouth Public Library

chapter eight
PESTILENCE AND WAR

The Mexican War ended in 1848. Far more devastating to Portsmouth and other Hampton Roads cities was a quiet invasion in 1855. The deadly enemy entered aboard a merchant ship bearing the patriotic name *Benjamin Franklin*. When the vessel docked near the Navy Yard in June and opened its hatches, it released *Aedes aegypti* mosquitoes, stowaways from a port in the West Indies. They carried yellow fever, the disease that had threatened to wipe out Philadelphia in 1793.

Portsmouth citizens had read sympathetically of plagues of cholera in New York City, the Middle West, and the Deep South, but had grown to think of themselves as almost immune to major epidemics. The blow was staggering mentally as well as physically when, in less than three months, the town lost more than 800 residents, about a tenth of the population of 8,626 shown by the federal census five years before. Norfolk lost an equal proportion. Many townsmen fled to the countryside. There were scarcely enough well persons to nurse the sick and bury the dead. Carts with warning yellow flags attached creaked through the streets with stacked corpses headed for mass burials. Physicians, nurses, ministers, and others—some from the area and some from distant places—served at great personal risk. Some sacrificed their lives.

Cold weather ended the epidemic, but no one knew then that the great sickness was traceable to the influx of mosquitoes from the West Indies. That connection was established at the turn of the century as the result of research by Dr. Walter Reed, the great Tidewater Virginia physician for whom the army medical center in Washington, D.C., is named.

Portsmouth rebounded quickly. In an age when every year brought word of a great epidemic somewhere, a community's reputation was not endangered even by a plague as severe as the one that had literally decimated the town. Just three years later, in 1858, Portsmouth was incorporated as a city. Thus it became, under the laws of Virginia regulating cities and counties, completely independent of Norfolk County. Portsmouth then began to share the courthouse with the county, the two entities composing their dockets so as to take turns in using the courtroom. Dissatisfaction with the system caused the county in 1859 to hold a referendum on removing the county seat to another location. The proposal was narrowly defeated and Portsmouth merchants continued to profit from the presence in their midst of Norfolk County's offices and courts. The federal census of 1860 showed that the city's population had risen to 9,496.

No less than fifteen hundred Portsmouth men were employed in the Navy Yard. Portsmouth's economic welfare and the personal safety of its citizens were still tied, even more intimately than those of most American communities, to questions of war and peace. But the prime threat was not foreign. This fact was dramatized in November 1859, when Portsmouth's National Grays, commanded by Capt. John E. Deans, were ordered to Harper's Ferry to suppress an insurrection.

John Brown, a crazed man wanted in Kansas for multiple murders with mutilation of the corpses, had led a band of eighteen men in seizing the Federal arsenal and armory at Harper's Ferry. It was then a Virginia town because West Virginia had not yet seceded from the

Commonwealth. Col. Robert E. Lee, assisted by young J. E. B. (Jeb) Stuart, captured Brown. The insurrectionist, an abolitionist, was tried and hanged by the federal government but some prominent Northerners honored him as a martyr. It was but one of many signs that the conflict between North and South was nearing explosive proportions. There was irony in the fact that two of the principal actors at Harper's Ferry, both then serving the Union, would soon be famous leaders of the Southern armies.

Reluctant Rebels

By February 1, 1861, South Carolina, Mississippi, Florida, Alabama, Georgia, Louisiana, and Texas—exercising a right that Virginia had obtained at the Constitutional Convention of 1787—seceded from the Union. Despite pressure from her Southern sisters, Virginia hesitated.

Virginians were loath to participate in the rending of a Union which they had done so much to build. Gov. John Letcher was a stout-hearted Unionist. Loyalty to the Union was even stronger in Portsmouth than in most of the Commonwealth. A large proportion of its citizens were employees of the federal government. Virginia leaders attempted to mediate between Washington and the seceding states, but when these efforts failed a state convention was called to consider secession. By large majorities, Portsmouth elected its two allotted delegates, James G. Holladay and Dr. William C. White, both pledged Unionists. On April 4 in Richmond the state convention voted eighty-eight to forty-five against secession. Many Portsmouth citizens relaxed a little on receipt of the reassuring news. But the convention remained in session to appraise fast moving developments. Then on April 15 President Lincoln called for seventy-five thousand volunteers from all the states in the Union, including Virginia, to subdue the rebels and punish South Carolina. Two days later, almost exactly reversing its earlier action, the Virginia convention voted eighty-eight to fifty-five for secession.

The ordinance of secession would be submitted to the people of Virginia in a referendum a month later, but the result was a foregone conclusion. A Confederate flag had already been raised over Craney Island. The day after the convention's vote in Richmond, Maj. Gen. William B. Taliaferro of the Virginia Guard and Captains Robert B. Pegram and Catesby ap R. Jones of the Virginia Navy arrived in Hampton Roads to organize the commonwealth's defenses.

Sadly, most Portsmouth residents reconciled themselves to severing cherished ties with the federal republic and apprehensively awaited the destruction that was inevitable because of the town's naval importance. About one-third of the inhabitants were black, some slaves and some free, but the whites felt little uneasiness on this score. Only a small minority of Portsmouth residents, or of Virginians for that matter, were slaveholders. And slavery played no commanding role in the economic and political rivalry of North and South. Some slaveholders in Portsmouth—as in Norfolk, Richmond, Norfolk County, and Princess Anne County—were themselves Negroes. When Union General John Charles Fremont, on August 30, 1861, ordered that the slaves of Missouri rebels be emancipated, Lincoln asked him to rescind the proclamation. When Fremont balked, Lincoln replied that the Civil War was "a war for a great national idea, the Union," and that "General Fremont should not have dragged the Negro into it." Lincoln, though personally opposed to slavery, had earlier expressed his willingness to preserve the nation half slave state and half free or even all slave if either condition were essential to preservation.

The Emancipation Proclamation of January 1, 1863, following the Preliminary Proclamation of September 22, 1862, stated that "all persons held as slaves within any State or designated part of a State, the people whereof shall then be in rebellion against the United States, shall be then, thenceforward, and forever free."

"In rebellion" were "the following, to wit: Arkansas, Texas, Louisiana, (except the Parishes of St. Bernard, Plaquemines, Jefferson, St. Johns, St. Charles, St. James, Ascension, Assumption, Terrebonne, Lafourche, St. Mary, St. Martin, and Orleans, including the city of New Orleans) Mississippi, Alabama, Florida, Georgia, South Carolina, and Virginia, (except the forty-eight counties designated as West Virginia, and also the counties of Berkley, Accomac, Northampton, Elizabeth City, York, Princess Anne and Norfolk, including the cities of Norfolk & Portsmouth); and which excepted parts are, for the present, left precisely as if this proclamation were not issued...."

This forbearance was in deference to strong Unionists, including Union generals such as Ulysses Grant, who were also slaveholders. Slavery was not completely abolished until the adoption of the Thirteenth Amendment to the Constitution in 1865.

On the eve of the Civil War Harper's Weekly *hailed the Navy Yard at Portsmouth as "one of the best in the United States" and cited its "granite dock which cost a million dollars." In the foreground is the* Pennsylvania, *anchored at the Yard as a receiving ship, which the New York magazine described as "the largest line-of-battle ship in the world."*
Photo courtesy Portsmouth Public Library

Up in Flames

Portsmouth was one of the first communities to feel the destructive power of the Federal forces. On April 20, 1861, they abandoned the Navy Yard, leaving it and eleven warships in flames that threatened to engulf the city itself. For Portsmouth people, the ordeal was made more nerve-wracking by the explosions that shook their homes.

The battle was soon to be joined. On the same day that the Federals abandoned the Navy Yard, Gov. John Letcher put the Third Virginia Regiment on active duty. Commanded by Col. James G. Hodges, the force included five Portsmouth companies: the Portsmouth Rifles, under Capt. John C. Owens; the Old Dominion Guard, under Capt. Edward Kearns; the National Grays, under Capt. John E. Deans; the Marion Rifles, under Capt. Johannes Watson; and the Portsmouth Light Artillery, under Capt. Cary F. Grimes. Other Portsmouth men served in companies from Norfolk and Norfolk County. As would be expected in a town with Portsmouth's seafaring traditions, others served in the Navy. Besides, five more companies were organized in the city.

Portsmouth troops who occupied the shipyard on April 21, under command of Capt. Robert P. Pegram of the Virginia Navy, found that what had been the largest shipyard in the United States was reduced to a smoking ruin. But the old stone drydock and some other facilities remained, and they salvaged 1,085 pieces of heavy naval ordnance, some of which were retained for local defense while the rest were dispersed to meet needs in other parts of the South.

On April 30 Federal warships began a blockade of Hampton Roads. A few days later Portsmouth Rifles, at Pig Point Battery (today the site of the Portsmouth campus of Tidewater Community College), fired upon and subdued the U.S. Revenue Cutter *Harriet Lane*.

Bloodier engagements were anticipated. Standing ready were the Portsmouth Sisters of Mercy, often saluted as "the first Confederate nursing unit."

Civilian spectators watch the burning of the Navy Yard in an unknown artist's record of the event.

Courtesy Portsmouth Public Library

Evacuating Union forces, on April 20, 1861, put the torch to the Navy Yard at Portsmouth. About five weeks after Harper's Weekly *published a picture of the facility as an example of United States naval might, one of its artists sketched this scene of its destruction (top) and of the burning of naval ships anchored there.*
Photo courtesy Portsmouth Public Library

Merrimac and Monitor

Responding to new threats posed by the fall to the Federals of Roanoke Island, North Carolina, Confederate President Jefferson Davis on February 27, 1862, declared martial law in both Portsmouth and Norfolk. He ordered plans for evacuation of women and children of the cities should they be besieged. The twenty thousand Confederate soldiers stationed in and around Portsmouth since November 1861 were protecting more than a strategically important location. The Navy Yard had been repaired with amazing celerity and held a secret that could do more than affect the course of the Civil War, that could change the naval history of the world.

Confederate Secretary of the Navy Stephen R. Mallory, aware of French and English interest in the potential of ironclad ships, conceived that such an innovation might rescue the Confederacy from its overwhelming disadvantages in naval power. Learning that the Navy Yard's naval constructor, John L. Porter, had designed an armed ship as early as 1846, Mallory summoned him to Richmond for a conference. This was on June 22, 1861. Both time and materials were lacking for construction of a new vessel to Porter's designs. He was therefore ordered to adapt his plans to converting the partly burned hull of the United States steam frigate *Merrimac (Merrimack)*, abandoned by the Federals when they burned the Navy Yard, into an armored ram. The result was a ship with decks virtually flush with the surface of the water and an armored casemate with sloping sides to deflect cannonballs. On the morning of March 8, 1862, the former *Merrimac*, rechristened the CSS *Virginia*, headed into Hampton Roads past beaches lined with spectators. Aboard was a crew of about 320, more from the Army than from the Navy. Several were black.

As the *Virginia* approached the massed Union warships, they fired mighty broadsides, but the cannonballs bounced off her iron sides like hail from a tin roof. The Confederate ship rammed and sank the fifty-gun USS *Cumberland*, then shelled the USS *Congress* till it caught fire and surrendered. As Virginius Dabney has written in *Virginia, the New Dominion*, "Naval warfare had been revolutionized in a single day, and the navies of the world were suddenly obsolete."

One member of President Lincoln's cabinet, perhaps frustrated by the apparent calm of his chief, insisted that the *Virginia* would be shelling the White House "before we leave this room." But the Union Navy already had its answer—an ironclad of its own. The newly constructed USS *Monitor*, with its revolving turret of iron, met the *Virginia* when she moved out again the next morning. For four hours the two ships dueled, sometimes locked in combat so close that the iron sides of one clanked against the other's. Neither could seriously injure the other. Eventually the *Monitor* withdrew toward the protection of Union guns at Fort Monroe and the *Virginia* returned to anchorage at Seawell's Point. Thus ended the first battle of ironclads in the history of western civilization. It was one of the most important events in the annals of war.

The *Virginia* made two more sorties into Hampton Roads on April 11, and May 8, and escaped challenge because of President Lincoln's personal order that "the *Monitor* be not too much exposed" until further appraisal of the situation in Hampton Roads. Meanwhile, events on land overtook the Confederate warhsip. On May 10 Confederate armed forces were forced to abandon Portsmouth and Norfolk and burned the Navy Yard. Federal troops occupied Norfolk that day and Portsmouth the next. The *Virginia*'s deep draft made escape up the James impossible. Determined not to surrender the vessel, her officers ran her aground near Craney Island and blew her up.

Some Southern cities occupied by Federal troops were lucky enough to be assigned humane, and even understanding, commanders. Such was not Portsmouth's good fortune. The occupation forces in Southeastern Virginia were under the command of Maj. Gen. Benjamin F. Butler, whose actions in the occupation of New Orleans had earned him the nickname "Beast." He also became known as "Spoon" Butler, some say unfairly, because of the rapid disappearance of silverware from private homes as he moved about the South. Butler was a political general, seldom successful in the field but adroit in climbing the ladder of command, who was little respected by many of his own men. When after the Civil War he touted his political candidacy with posters calling him "the hero of Five Forks," a small engagement in Virginia, an irreverent veteran of his service added "and the Lord knows how many silver spoons."

Under Butler's rule in Portsmouth, much private property was confiscated and some families were placed

The USS Steam Frigate Merrimac is shown before its partial burning during Federal evacuation of the Navy Yard. Photo courtesy Portsmouth Public Library

THE NAVAL ENGAGEMENT BETWEEN THE MERRIMAC AND THE MONITOR AT HAMPTON ROADS ON THE 9TH OF MARCH 1862.

The USS Monitor challenges the CSS Virginia (Merrimac) on March 9, 1862. Craney Island is the first island near the far shore. Norfolk is part of the land mass beyond the flag of the Craney Island battery. Portsmouth, across the Elizabeth River from Norfolk, lies to the right of Craney Island and behind a line of trees. The Virginia is virtually surrounded by Union ships. At left midground, with a plume of smoke pouring from its stack, is a French man-of-war observing the drama. Photo courtesy Portsmouth Public Library

under house arrest with armed guards at their doors. A Confederate flag was spread on the ground at the approach to the ferry so that those wishing to board would have to tread upon the emblem for which relatives were risking, and sometimes losing, their lives. For praying for the president of the Confederacy, the Reverend J. H. D. Wingfield, assistant rector of Trinity Episcopal Church, was jailed in Norfolk and then at Fort Monroe. Some Northern newspapers condemned the inhumanity and folly of Butler's methods.

Heartened by the brilliant victories of Generals Robert E. Lee and Thomas J. (Stonewall) Jackson over Union forces far larger than their own, and clinging to the possibility of English or French intervention, Portsmouth citizens desperately hoped for rescue by Confederate successes nearer home. But the economic, industrial, and naval strength of the Federals, even more than their formidable superiority in numbers, led to Lee's surrender at Appomattox on April 9, 1865. When many Southern communities then looked to Federal occupation with dread of the unknown, it was already an old story to Portsmouth. The city's record was a strange one. It had been ardently Unionist even after the war had begun, its representatives had supported every serious move to mediate the quarrel, and the city had accepted secession only after Virginia had been ordered to furnish troops against her sister states and faced the prospect of having Federal troops march across her borders. Yet Portsmouth had paid a higher price than some Southern communities that had been hotbeds of secession. She had endured a harsh occupation for nearly three years and had sent 1,400 men—a large proportion of her adult male population—into the Confederate forces. Of these, about 230 had died in service.

Many Portsmouth men spared by war were lost in the peace. Under the military rule following surrender, the town was in debt to the extent of $300,000 and its treasury was literally empty. Many of its citizens were almost literally penniless. By January 1866 the Navy Yard was being restored and gave employment to 620 people, but former soldiers and sailors of the Confederacy were barred from jobs, as were all who had furnished supplies to the rebels. They could not look to reform by ballot because they were disenfranchised. Under these circumstances, many who had been sustained on the battlefield and on long marches by the dream of returning home now reluctantly left their city.

Reconstruction in Virginia as a formal policy lasted from March 2, 1867, to January 26, 1870, during which time the Commonwealth was designated Military District No. 1 and was subject to a military governor.

■

John L. Porter, Portsmouth native and naval constructor in both the United States and Confederate navies, who helped to make international history when he designed the conversion of the USS Merrimac *into the CSS* Virginia. *Photo courtesy Portsmouth Public Library*

The giant CSS Virginia (Merrimac) and the tiny Monitor clash in battle in this news engraving from the period. At times the two ships are so close that their iron sides clang together.
Courtesy Richard A. Horwege

The bullet-riddled smokestack of the exploded CSS Virginia lies on the beach at Craney Island.
Photo courtesy Portsmouth Public Library

Ruins of the Navy Yard were photographed during the Civil War, possibly by James Gardner, son of Alexander Gardner, assistant to famed photographer Mathew Brady. Despite widespread destruction by both Federals and Confederates, eleven buildings of the facility have survived to this day. The lone human figure in the desolate scene is believed to be Alfred R. Waud, noted illustrator for Harper's Weekly.
Photo courtesy Public Affairs Office, Naval Shipyard

The screw frigate USS Franklin *anchors off Portsmouth's Navy Yard about 1878. Berkley and Norfolk are in the background. Photo courtesy Portsmouth Public Library*

chapter nine
A NEW ERA

On April 30, 1870, less than three months after the end of military rule in Virginia, General Lee visited the city on his tour of the South. The white-bearded general stepped off the Seaboard and Roanoke Railroad train and, with the dignity of an Anglo-Saxon king, walked with his escort toward the ferry wharf. A large crowd of men and women cheered him and the thunder of artillery sent echoes bouncing off nearby walls. A small brass cannon was fired in salute from a group of young men, some wearing the classic fire helmets of early days, others the bread-loaf helmets of the police. As Lee stepped aboard the ferry, rockets and roman candles were fired by Portsmouth citizens and cannon boomed from the Norfolk docks.

Less than six months later Robert E. Lee was dead. Northern as well as Southern newspapers saluted the great leader who had worked as energetically to heal the nation's wounds as he had to lead the South's armies in battle. There was drama in the fact that his life, symbolic of the best in the old South, ended in the same year that Virginia resumed her place in the Union. Found among the general's papers after his death was a message: "History teaches us to hope."

In the days that followed, Portsmouth recalled that it was part of the great world, took pride once again in its Navy Yard, and, while honoring the Confederate heroes in its midst, turned its face to the future. The city was briefly in the international spotlight in January and February 1877, when the Grand Dukes Alexis and Constantine, heirs to the Russian throne, and Prince Oblinski paid a two-month visit to Hampton Roads. Excitement was touched off on the morning of January 13 when the frigate *Svetlana*, commanded by Rear Admiral Boutakoff, entered the Elizabeth River. It reached a peak on February 8, when prominent Portsmouth citizens attended a ball at the Navy Yard in honor of the royal guests. The zenith was maintained through the next big event several days later, a *matinee dansante* at which the grand dukes were hosts aboard their ship. Long after the Russians' departure, some young ladies always referred to the Grand Duke Constantine as "the darling little fellow." The town fathers were so caught up in exotic glamour that they named one street Cossack and another Muscovite. Later, civic pride and patriotism reasserted themselves and Cossack Street became Portsmouth Boulevard while Muscovite became Madison.

True progress was measured in developments of more lasting import. By 1870 Portsmouth's population was 10,590, or 1,094 more than on the eve of the Civil War, and by 1880 it had risen to 11,390. The city's first *public* high school held its first graduation exercises in 1885. In the same year the Portsmouth Street Railway won a franchise to operate horse-drawn cars, and in 1901 the first cars were replaced with electric streetcars that whined along the tracks and spit blue fire when they rounded corners. In January 1889, electric lights replaced the gas lights that had illuminated Portsmouth homes and, since 1854, streetlights "on nights that the almanac predicted no moon."

The city acquired a new industry in response to the needs of Norfolk County truck farmers, for whom business was booming as coastal steamers began transporting their crops to Washington, Baltimore, and points north. The

Portsmouth Basket Works, creating more than a hundred new jobs, was founded in 1889. By 1890 the population had climbed to 13,268, and the city's newspapers, cooperating with efforts to attract outside capital, described Portsmouth as "one of the liveliest towns in the state" and submitted in evidence:

> Compare Portsmouth of today with the mud hole it was ten years ago. Nicely paved and graded streets have taken the place of the old muddy roads. The old street pump has given way to the Portsmouth and Suffolk Water Works. The mails are gathered up and delivered by carriers. The city railroad starting from the ferry wharf has three lines: one via Crawford to the Navy Yard and through Fourth and Court Streets. A second via Court, North and Green to the Naval Hospital, while the main line goes beyond the city limits to the thriving little suburb of Scottsville. Portsmouth has a nice City Hall, containing mayor's office, police station and fire engine rooms, with armories for her military companies in the upper stories and surmounted by a fine illuminated clock, court house, post office, three public schools, fourteen churches, and many stores, warehouses and private residences.

Of course, many residents thought of their city primarily as a pleasant place to live, with beaches, boat clubs, amateur theatricals, concerts, and, just across the Elizabeth River, the various attractions of the larger city of Norfolk. And a few occasionally sampled the pleasures of metropolitan centers elsewhere in the United States and abroad.

Steamboat Romance

For those not able or inclined to travel far, the Chesapeake Bay offered special charms in one of its most romantic periods, the era of steamboating. What the stern-wheeled steamer with its great white wedding cake architecture had been to the Mississippi, the gleaming, multi-decked bay steamboat was to the Chesapeake. From Baltimore, Washington, and Alexandria the sidewheelers moved down the bay, stopping at innumerable rural wharves on the Eastern Shore and on the mainland, their imperious whistles setting whole communities astir with a bustle to match the agitation of usually quiet waters roiled to a froth as white as the shining vessels themselves.

Sunlight glancing from brass rails dimmed even the gilt splendor of the huge letters proclaiming a proud name. Shoulder-shaking laughter, rich and dark and sweet as sorghum, gurgled from sweating dock hands and crewmen laboring under the supercilious eyes of a bland-faced waiter who, resplendent in white coat and secure in his elevation on deck, looked down on them from under drooping lids.

Up the gangway and up the steps was a huge mirror reflecting the glory of a red-carpeted saloon with a piano less musical than the boat whistle. There might be a better piano at home and the parlor that housed it might be furnished with a quiet taste more refined than the garish red and shining brass of the steamboat. But that fact did not matter.

The steamboat was Mark Twain's Mississippi come to Tidewater; it was Bagdad compressed between sidewheels; it was the great world floating up to the dock at Portsmouth or Norfolk, or even Concord Wharf, Merry Point, Deltaville, and many another waterside village in the Chesapeake country.

Naval Might

Much larger vessels than the bay's steamboats claimed Portsmouth's attention in the last decade of the nineteenth century. Appropriately, the local Navy Yard, which had made world history by constructing the ironclad CSS *Virginia*, launched in 1892 two of the first steel-hulled ships of the modern United States Navy, the USS *Raleigh*, a cruiser, and the USS *Texas*, the Navy's first battleship.

In 1893 an International Navy Review celebrated somewhat belatedly the four hundredth anniversary of the discovery of America by Columbus in 1492. The World's Columbian Exposition was held in Chicago but the accompanying naval rendezvous was in Hampton Roads. Reproductions of the *Nina*, the *Pinta*, and the *Santa Maria* sailed among the warships of nine nations. British, Italian, and Russian ships were visible from Portsmouth. Views of all were available to those who

A small brass cannon fired in salute to General Robert E. Lee when he visited Portsmouth on April 30, 1870, claims the attention of eight-year-old Ramona Hamby. Today the cannon is in Portsmouth's Naval Shipyard Museum.

An aerial view of downtown Portsmouth was sketched, as if from the crow's nest of a ship at anchor, for Pollock's Sketchbook, *published in 1886.*

ventured out in small boats. Some of the warships had three masts and some had three smokestacks. One of the great transitions of history was manifest in the parade.

The Spanish warships that were welcomed to Hampton Roads in 1893 would have met a quite different reception five years later. In April 1898 the United States and Spain went to war over Cuba. Fitzhugh Lee, a former governor of Virginia, nephew of Robert E. Lee, and once a Confederate major general, became a symbol of national unity when he went to war in the uniform of a federal major general of volunteers. Many Virginians followed his example. Portsmouth was well represented. The war was brief but dangerous. More men died from bad beef sold to the Army than from enemy bullets. Two great American heroes emerged from the war, Commodore (later Admiral) George Dewey, victor of Manila Bay, and Col. Theodore Roosevelt, whose Rough Riders won fame at San Juan Hill. A Spanish cruiser, the *Reina Mercedes* entered Portsmouth's Navy Yard as a prize of war and Adm. Pascual Cervera, commander of the Spanish fleet in Cuba, became, like others of his countrymen, a patient in Portsmouth Naval Hospital

In The Vanguard

In 1900 Portsmouth had doubled its area to 1.4 square miles since the federal census of 1890, and its population had jumped to 17,427. In that year there were no automobiles or trucks in Virginia. In 1902, Dr. George Carr became the first automobile owner in Portsmouth and one of the first in the state. His vehicle was a single-cylinder Oldsmobile steered with a lever and bearing a close family resemblance to the buggy. Oldsmobile, manufacturer of the first commercially successful American automobile, had sold 115 cars in the United States in 1901.

Soon the motorized buggies with the big lanterns were frightening horses at every crossroads in Tidewater Virginia as motorists, no less alien and formidable in dusters and goggles, dismounted in vain attempts to reassure the panicked beasts.

Local transportation of all kinds was taxed by a heavy burden in 1907 when the Jamestown Exposition, a world's fair commemorating the three hundredth anniversary of America's first permanent English settlement, brought people from all parts of the United States and some foreign countires to Hampton Roads. As Jamestown Island was too small to accommodate an international exposition, the event was staged at Seawell's (Sewell's) Point, then in Norfolk County. (Norfolk Naval Base is now at that site.) The exposition itself was not a profitable enterprise but it proved a splendid advertisement for Hampton Roads and a begetter of new businesses as well as a stimulus to the old. Thomas J. Wertenbaker wrote in 1931, "The Jamestown Exposition was the forerunner of the greater Hampton Roads of the twentieth century." Portsmouth had a part in the planning—one of its citizens, J. T. Wood, was a vice president of the corporation—and the city shared in the benefits.

The presidency (1901-1909) of Theodore Roosevelt, a big Navy man, saw rapid expansion of that service, climaxed by the sending of the Great White Fleet around the world in 1907. The president's policies resulted in impressive growth of the Navy Yard. When Roosevelt visited Portsmouth in 1906, he received a hero's welcome.

In 1909, by the annexation of Scottsville and Prentis Place, Portsmouth had increased in area from 1.4 to 2.4 square miles. The federal census of 1910 showed that the city's population had increased to 33,190, a gain of 90.4 percent in a decade. By 1915 Portsmouth's population was about 38,000. Soon people were wearing lapel buttons saying "Portsmouth, 40,000 and Still Growing."

In that same year the National Municipal League adopted the city manager plan of government as the basis of its model charter for municipalities. The city manager system had originated in Staunton, Virginia, in 1908. Sumter, South Carolina, had adopted it in 1912, and in 1913 Dayton, Ohio, had become the first large city to try it. Portsmouth adopted it in 1916. After 1918 there was a rush for adoption among many American cities, and some foreign municipalities, but Portsmouth was in the vanguard. The most important feature of the new system was the employment of a manager whose position under the council was analogous to that of a corporate manager operating under a board of directors. Portsmouth's first city manager was T. B. Schertzer.

city managers of portsmouth

1. Tyrell B. Shertzer reported to work on January 2, 1917. Resignation requested June 25, 1917; terminated as city manager July 31, 1917.
2. W. B. Bates, July 28, 1917.
3. J. P. Jervey, 1920-1926.
4. Frank C. Hanrahan, 1927-1932.
5. Harold B. Anderson, 1932-1934.
6. Edward B. Hawks, 1935-1936.
7. Charles F. Harper, 1937-1940.
8. M. E. Haug, 1940-1941.
9. Arthur S. Owens, 1942-1949.
10. W. Guy Ansel, 1949-1951.
11. I. G. Vass, 1951-1958.
12. Aubrey P. Johnson, Jr., 1958-1974.
13. Phineas Horton, 1974-1976.
14. Robert T. Williams, 1976-1980.
15. G. Robert House, 1981-1982.
16. George L. Hanbury II, 1982-.

Dr. Antonio L. Bilisoly (left) stands in front of his pharmacy, 234 High Street (at Middle) in 1896. A former surgeon with the Confederate States Army, he abandoned his medical practice after the Civil War. Standing next to him is Charles McGinley. The third figure is unidentified.
Photo courtesy Portsmouth Public Library

R. W. Chapman Company, 310 High Street, still in business as Chapman's Jewelers, presented this appearance to its customers in 1890. Note the gaslight fixtures and, beside a handsome display case on the right, the obligatory brass spittoon. Mr. Chapman, the proprietor, stands third from the left. E. F. Jakeman is second from the left and William Deans is on the far right behind the counter.
Photo courtesy Portsmouth Public Library

Dennis Sullivan (probably the central figure), as blacksmith, carriage maker, and wheelright, performed a vital service in the 1890s. His establishment was at 600-608 Middle Street on the southwest corner of Middle and King streets. Cary Colliers (in apron) is at right.
Photo courtesy Portsmouth Public Library

This is the earliest known photograph of downtown Portsmouth, looking west up High Street from Crawford Street after a snowfall in 1871 or 1872. The photographer is not known. One is tempted to speculate that it was the proprietor of Howlett's Photography, whose sign appears so prominently in the right foreground. The fourth building on the left, a high basement or Bristol-built house, was the home of the Reverend Richard Cleveland, pastor of Portsmouth's First Presbyterian Church, but better known to history as the father of President Grover Cleveland.
Photo courtesy Portsmouth Public Library

Things were busy in West Norfolk in 1895 at the West Norfolk Lumber Company (right) and at the Atlantic and Danville Railroad Terminal (above).
Photos courtesy Portsmouth Public Library

The downtown Portsmouth waterfront looks more peaceful than busy in this 1892 photograph. The inset shows the Craney Island lighthouse.
Photo courtesy Portsmouth Public Library

ESTABLISHED 1839.
ETHEREDGE & BROOKS,
(Successors to NIEMEYER, ETHEREDGE & BROOKS.)

HIGH ST. & CITY WHARF, PORTSMOUTH, VA.

Cotton Factors and General Commission Merchants,

for the sale of Peanuts, Dried Fruit, all Southern Products, and dealers in Builders' and Agricultural Lime and Plaster, Cement and Hay. Wholesale Dealers in COALS of all kinds. Peruvian and Standard Guanos for Truck, Cotton, Peanuts, Corn, &c. Liberal Advances made on Consignments or Transits.

GEORGE L. NEVILLE,
Wholesale and Retail Dealer in

Domestic and Foreign Hardware, Ship Chandlery, Iron, Steel and Metals, Paints, Oils and Glass, and General Contractor for Naval Supplies.

602 & 604 CRAWFORD STREET, PORTSMOUTH, VA.

[277]

G. ARMSTRONG & SON,

Crawford Street, foot of South St.,

PORTSMOUTH, VA.

SAW AND PLANING MILL.

MANUFACTURERS, WHOLESALE AND RETAIL DEALERS IN

Lumber, Laths, Shingles, Posts.

Kiln-Dried Flooring and Ceiling a Specialty.

VEGETABLE AND FRUIT BOXES.

BILL TIMBER AND KILN-DRIED LUMBER

A SPECIALTY.

☞ Portsmouth City Water for Sale.

[276]

In the age of horse and carriages, the dead as well as the living sometimes rode in style through the streets of Portsmouth. From Our Twin Cities of the Nineteenth Century: Norfolk and Portsmouth, *1887-1888.*

Advertisements in Our Twin Cities of the Nineteenth Century: Norfolk and Portsmouth, *published in 1887-1888 under the editorship of Robert W. Lamb, afford glimpses of the commercial life of the period.*

D. V. GASKINS.   CHAS. H. STURTEVANT.

Gaskins & Sturtevant,

Funeral Directors AND Embalmers

610 MIDDLE STREET, PORTSMOUTH, VA.

B. H. OWENS,
DEALER IN FIRST-CLASS
Staple and Fancy Dry Goods.

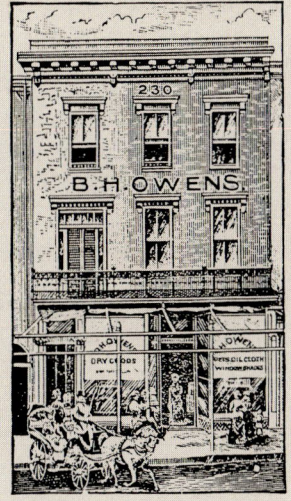

We keep no old stock, believing the first loss is always the best, and Small Profits and Quick Sales the only proper maxim of a Successful Business. Our Stock and Prices are kept conformable to the times, adding whatever is New and Desirable, and our long experience in business, with a knowledge of the wants of the community, enables us not only to buy our Goods at the Closest Figures, but to offer you just the Goods you want at the Lowest Prices. Our Stock comprises

Dress Goods, Cloaks, Shawls, Cashmeres, Notions, Hosiery, Gloves, Corsets, Ladies', Gents' and Children's Underwear, Cloths, Cassimeres, Collars, Cravats, Carpets, Oil Cloths, Mattings Window Shades and Cornices.

OUR PRICES GUARANTEED.
No. 230 HIGH STREET,
ESTABLISHED 1852.
PORTSMOUTH, VA.
[282]

PHILLIPS & NASH,
DEALERS IN
DRY GOODS and NOTIONS,

CARPETS, OIL CLOTHS, MATTINGS, &c.
Kirn Building, 229 High Street, Portsmouth, Va.

A franchise to operate horse-drawn streetcars in Portsmouth was granted in 1885 and vehicles like the one behind High Street workers in this photograph soon appeared on the city's thoroughfares.
Photo courtesy Portsmouth Public Library

Another electric streetcar approaches from the east in this old photograph of High Street between Middle and Crawford streets.
Photo courtesy Portsmouth Public Library

In 1901 electric streetcars, like the one more than a block away in this photograph looking west on High Street, replaced the horsedrawn streetcars.
Photo courtesy Everett Harrison

Despite Portsmouth's boast in 1890 that "Nicely paved and graded streets have taken the place of old muddy roads," some of the mudholes survived well past the turn of the century as evidenced in this 1911 photograph of South Street Road west of Chestnut Street.
Photo courtesy Portsmouth Public Library

Principal downtown streets were neatly paved by the turn of the century and well maintained thereafter as shown in this view of High Street from the ferry (above), and looking down High Street toward the ferries from the intersection of High and Court streets (left). The classical structure on the right is the post office. On the left is the Ocean House hotel.
Photos courtesy Everett Harrison

A Portsmouth native gaining national fame in the 1890s was Sissieretta Jones (c. 1868-1933), who, after her 1888 singing debut on the New York stage, was dubbed the "Black Patti" in reference to opera star Adelina Patti. Her concerts included a command performance at the White House and her admirers charged that only racial prejudice denied her a Metropolitan debut. Increasing segregation in both the North and the South wiped out most appearances before mixed or white audiences after 1895. Then she organized the Black Patti Troubadors, who for nineteen seasons entertained black audiences with a pastiche of comedy, art songs, opera, folk songs, and gospel music. The Republic of Haiti presented her a gold medal. Portsmouth blacks remembered her as Matilda Sissieretta Joyner Jones, a little girl whose first public performance was in a local church. In 1976 a "Landmark of American Music Plaque" honoring her was presented to the Portsmouth Public Library by the National Music Council, the Virginia Federation of Music Clubs, and Exxon Corporation.
Photo courtesy Portsmouth Public Library

A large poster advertising a performance by "Black Patti," Sissieretta Jones, appears in 1910 in a black neighborhood of her native city. In this view of the west side of Chestnut Street, looking from Clifford Street toward South Street, the advertisement is midway between the central tree and the next one to the right.
Photo courtesy Portsmouth Public Library

*To many in the early 1880s, Swimming Point seemed an idyllic neighborhood. The porches and tree-shaded lawns afforded beautiful views of the harbor. Boathouses sheltered pleasure craft. All the attractions of downtown were nearby. Near the center of the shoreline in this picture is the turreted mansion of R.T.K. Bain, later the home of Goodrich Hatton, prominent attorney and Portsmouth's delegate to the Virginia Constitutional Convention of 1901-02.
Photo courtesy Portsmouth Public Library*

*Though the slush may look forbidding, the ice-and-snow-covered trees have an ethereal beauty in this 1895 photo of the chalet-like Milligan House on Court Street. To the left is the First Presbyterian Church, whose congregation had been served by the Reverend Richard Cleveland, father of Grover Cleveland who was then President of the United States. The site of the Milligan House is occupied today by the Portsmouth Public Library.
Photo courtesy Portsmouth Public Library*

*Portsmouth's 1846 Court House had an iron fence and railed steps in 1895. The grounds wore a more formal look than in earlier times and buildings were crowding the borders of the courtyard. Long gone were the days of the 1850s when carts and covered wagons still gathered in neighborly fashion and Indians riding in from the countryside competed in shooting matches with pennies as targets. The Dutch-roof frame house at the left was the home of Dr. Virginius B. Bilisoly, later the site of the Norfolk County Clerk's office. Col. William H. Stewart, historian of Norfolk County, once had his law office on the ground floor of the Bilisoly home. To the left of this dwelling was the home of V. O. Cassell. The Portsmouth City Council, School Board, Board of Health, and Police Commissioners met in the southeast corner of the Courthouse. County officers were housed in the same building.
Photo courtesy Portsmouth Public Library*

Miss Esther Wilson, popularly known as Miss Essie, Portsmouth's first public librarian, poses on September 21, 1918, with her nephew Claudius Murdaugh.
Photo courtesy Portsmouth Public Library

The residence of Franklin D. and Cora Mapp Gill, at Middle and Glasgow streets, about 1892, represented the height of fashionable American Gothic elegance. The Gothic tracery of the eaves above the two-story bay windows recalls the Moorish filigree of the Alhambra. The house is in an excellent state of preservation today.
Photo courtesy Portsmouth Public Library

Two Emmerson homes, a Victorian house with conical tower, and (next door) a hip-roofed dwelling built about 1785, graced the 400 block of High Street in 1910. The Emmersons have been prominent in Portsmouth since the eighteenth century. To the left is the wall of Trinity Churchyard. Today the Commodore Theater occupies the site of the Emmerson homes.
Photo courtesy Portsmouth Public Library

The William J. Davis Palace Stable, 607-609 Middle Street, was described by the Norfolk Virginian in 1897 as the finest establishment of its kind in either Portsmouth or Norfolk. Built in 1894 to replace an earlier stable founded by Mr. Davis in 1883, its two-story facade was fifty-seven feet wide and the building was two hundred feet long. The ground floor included an office, stalls for one hundred horses, and a "well-equipped bicycle room." The second floor was used for the storage of vehicles, but also included an "elegantly equipped ladies' parlor and waiting room" and washrooms. Among vehicles for rent were "Berlin and Manhattan coaches, landaus, drags, and traps of the most elegant design and finish."
Photo from the Norfolk Virginian

J. & E. Mahoney, Rectifier and Wholesale Liquor Dealers, had offices and a warehouse at the southeast corner of High and Water streets. They had a thriving business until the Mapp Act required the closing of all saloons in Virginia on or before November 1, 1916. At that time two hundred businessmen in Portsmouth and Norfolk County applied for licenses to sell soft drinks. The thick-walled structure later housed the Portsmouth Star, Portsmouth's leading newspaper, now part of the Ledger-Star. Room was found on the second floor for the Portsmouth Police Court.
Photo courtesy Portsmouth Public Library

The new market did not replace more informal marketing arrangements. Witness the Old fish market carrying on in 1895 under a big "Bull Durham" sign in the 100 block of County Street (left), and the line of market tents and wagons extending from South Street along Crawford Street to High Street (above).
Photos courtesy Portsmouth Public Library

The Seaboard Market and Armory, an imposing building with castellated towers that fed some youngsters' dreams of medieval romance, was completed in 1893 at the northwest corner of Crawford and South streets. The structure was razed in 1945.
Photo courtesy Portsmouth Public Library

Three photographs from 1901 show sellers of produce arriving at the south end of Middle Street (top), salesmen by their wagons on South Street (middle), and a woman and a young girl, each with a bag in hand, shopping for groceries. Photos courtesy Portsmouth Public Library

The Old Kirn Building, seen here in 1893, was built by Henry Kirn in 1887 at the southeast corner of High and Middle streets. It was not as handsome as the New Kirn Building, but it was important to the city. The ground floor housed Merchants' and Farmers' Bank and other businesses while offices and the YMCA occupied the second. The third floor, known as Kirn Hall, was the scene of amateur theatricals and the annual supper balls of the Portsmouth Assembly. This floor was destroyed by fire on August 1, 1930.
Photo courtesy Portsmouth Public Library

Leaders of Churchland's landed gentry pose outside the local Grange Hall, circa 1900. Standing, left to right, are John T. Griffin, Wright Bruce Carney, Stephen Barnaby Carney, and Henry Kirn. Seated, left to right, are Mrs. Griffin and Mrs. Josepha Kingman. Mr. Griffin was a founder and president of Merchants and Farmers Bank of Portsmouth, since absorbed by Dominion Bank. The two Carneys were representative of separate branches of a family prominent in Norfolk County since 1664. Wright Carney was a bank director and influential business leader. Stephen Carney, a railroad director and developer of West Norfolk, was for eight years chairman of the Norfolk County Board of Supervisors and later postmaster of Norfolk. Mrs. Kingman, who lived past her hundredth birthday, managed her extensive business affairs almost to the day of her death. Mr. Kirn, reputedly the richest man in the county, is memorialized with his wife in Norfolk's Kirn Library, made possible by the gifts of his philanthropic children. At the time of this picture, Portsmouth's Churchland suburb was one of the wealthiest agricultural communities in the United States and its truck farming heavily supported the city's basket manufacturing. Later Churchland was annexed by Portsmouth.
Photo courtesy Norfolk County Historical Society

Jno. T. Griffin, President.   J. H. Toomer, Cashier.

MERCHANTS' & FARMERS' BANK,
PORTSMOUTH, VA.

COMMENCED BUSINESS DECEMBER 1, 1885.

Capital, $51,500.   Surplus, 13,000.

INTERIOR VIEW OF MERCHANTS' AND FARMERS' BANK.

Unsurpassed facilities for the accommodation of Customers and for the transaction of all their banking business.

Careful and prompt attention given to Collections, which are remitted for at lowest rates.

Safe Deposit Boxes, for the security of Stocks, Bonds, Deeds and other valuables, against fire and burglars, for rent at reasonable rates.

*Shortly after Merchants' and Farmers' Bank opened its doors in 1885, its $51,500 capitalization was a matter for boastful advertising. It soon became one of the two or three most prestigious banks in the Portsmouth-Norfolk County area. Note the gaslight chandeliers and wall sconce (left), fancy cashier's cage, and tile floors. A shiny brass cuspidor (lower right corner) was de rigueur in high-toned financial institutions of the period.
From* Our Twin Cities of the Nineteenth Century: Norfolk and Portsmouth, 1887-1888

*Train cars like this one ran onto sidings on individual estates in the Churchland area to load produce for Northern markets. For the wealthy planters it was a counterpart to the kind of service enjoyed by their eighteenth-century ancestors when sailing ships bound for great ports stopped at individual wharves.
Photo courtesy Portsmouth Public Library*

The dark-hulled Old Dominion steamer Hamilton *passes Hospital Point inbound from New York City in this 1910 photograph. A two-masted sailing ship can be seen in the left background.*
Photo from the Emmerson Collection, Portsmouth Public Library

The Old Dominion Line steamer Luray *was a jaunty addition to the local scene in 1895. Its tall smokestack, huge sidewheels and double decks made it stand out from other harbor craft.*
Photo courtesy Portsmouth Public Library

The Old Bay Line steamer Florida *is tied up at the Seaboard's passenger wharf in this 1915 photo, but the smoke from her stack suggests that her departure is imminent. The Seaboard Building, now No. One High Street, is prominent in the background. To the right is the Portsmouth Star Building, which also housed some Seaboard offices.*
Seaboard Air Line Railway photo

The USS Texas, the Navy's first battleship, was launched at Portsmouth's Navy Yard in 1892. The few spectators seem remarkably nonchalant just before the event.
Photo courtesy Portsmouth Naval Shipyard Museum

This engraving of President Theodore Roosevelt is a souvenir of the Jamestown Tercentennial Exposition.
Courtesy Richard A. Horwege

When President Theodore Roosevelt visited Portsmouth on Memorial Day in 1906, the Post Office (classical building in center) and Town Hall (cupola with clock) were decked in bunting, sailors marched down Court Street past the Confederate Monument, and crowds thronged the intersection with High Street.
Photo courtesy Portsmouth Public Library

President Theodore Roosevelt doffs his hat to well-wishers at a bunting-bedecked house at Court and Bart streets.
Photo courtesy Portsmouth Public Library

An early touring car pauses in Court Street beside the Confederate monument, near the intersection with High Street. To the right is the Monroe Hotel, successor to the Ocean House. The spire of Court Street Baptist Church rises behind the trees.
Photo courtesy Everett Harrison

A monument to Portsmouth veterans of the Spanish-American War, originally erected in the City Park, stands guard now over the median strip in Crawford Parkway.
Photo by Ramona H. Mapp

J. H. Green, veteran seaman of the Spanish-American War, proudly wears his medals as Portsmouth pays tribute to its patriots.
Photo from the Rodgers Collection, Portsmouth Public Library

Dr. George Carr became Portsmouth's first automobile owner in 1901. For a long time motor cars were greatly outnumbered by horsedrawn vehicles as in this early postcard where a lone auto, second vehicle from right, appears among its more traditional counterparts on High Street.
Photo courtesy Everett Harrison

The Portsmouth Retail Merchants Association in the early 1900s boasted fifteen members, some of whom would become prominent leaders in the city and beyond. From left to right, they were: front row— A. B. Jarvis, T. S. Lawrence, Nathan Levy, and William Chapman. Second row— William Hodges Baker, B. F. Hofheimer, John A. Morris, a Mr. Armantrout, and E. Anthony. Back row— S. T. Hanger; W. Maupin, Jr.; W. F. Robertson; J. W. Booth; and E. D. Clements. The surname of the man on the far right is torn from the photograph, but the first part of his name is "Maurice A."
Photo courtesy Portsmouth Public Library

Church and state meet in this 1910 view of Court Street at the intersection with High Street. The classic facade with Tuscan columns belongs to an agency of the United States government, the Post Office. The cupola of the Town Hall looms above an old house sheltering the offices of T. A. Bain. Nestled between that building and the Post Office is an awninged booth, apparently dispensing fruit and vegetables.
Photo courtesy Portsmouth Public Library

A little girl crosses the street where two men talk beneath the balcony on the northwest corner of South and Chestnut streets, a black neighborhood where businesses and residences met in 1912. Photo from the Emmerson Collection, courtesy of Portsmouth Public Library

The National Printing Company, at High and Green streets, included in 1915 a stationery department and book bindery. The company is still in business on High Street. For decades local stationers had sold magazines. Their advertisements reveal that, at least as early as the 1870s, Portsmouth readers enjoyed not only a wide array of American magazines but also the leading literary journals of Great Britain and some French publications. Photo courtesy Portsmouth Public Library

Bicycles, carriages, wagons, and pedestrians are still the predominant traffic in this view of High Street looking west from below Court Street. In right foreground is the Ocean House, future site of The Famous, a ladies' fashions store drawing customers from other Hampton Roads communities and North Carolina. The columned portico on the far side of Court Street belongs to the 1846 Court House. The next visible building is the future home of the Colony Theater. The spire rising behind the Court House is the steeple of Monumental Methodist Church. The steeple to the left is that of St. Paul's Catholic Church. Photo courtesy Portsmouth Public Library

Some people in 1910-1912 kept their boats near (left) the Boat House on Hospital Point while others kept theirs in homelier surroundings at (top) the foot of Hunter's Lane, behind the east side of the first block of Court Street. Sportsman Harry Richardson, in his "Naptha" launch in this 1908 photograph (right), patronized the Portsmouth Boat Club. The second photo is from the Emmerson Collection; all are courtesy of the Portsmouth Public Library

Residential shores of Scott's Creek, West Park View, are seen here in 1911. The waterfront house at the left is the home of Hubert Ward.
Photo from the Emmerson Collection, courtesy Portsmouth Public Library

Strollers on Court Street pause beside the cemetery wall at Trinity Episcopal Church to chat on a sunny afternoon in 1910. Note the fire hydrant in right foreground.
Photo courtesy Portsmouth Public Library

3.

Workboats tied up at the wharf of a Scott's Creek oyster house in 1911 were probably operated by Ayers Seafood. Pinners Point is in the background. Photo from the Emmerson Collection, courtesy Portsmouth Public Library

Looking startlingly like a painting by Georges Seurat, this 1912 photograph shows the wooden bridge leading from the north end of Dinwiddie Street to Swimming Point and the Naval Hospital. Photo courtesy Portsmouth Public Library

Gen. Wendell Cushing Neville was Portsmouth's most famous hero of World War I. Having already seen service in the Spanish-American War, the Boxer Rebellion, Nicaragua, and Vera Cruz, Neville fought in France as colonel of the Fifth Regiment of United States Marines. His courage and ability won him promotion to brigadier general. On March 15, 1929, he became commandant of the Marine Corps. Marine Corps photo, courtesy Portsmouth Public Library

chapter ten
WORLD WAR I

The efficiency of Portsmouth's new government was severely tested as the coming of World War I made the city a boomtown. The war had opened in Europe in 1914, but President Woodrow Wilson, popular in Portsmouth as the eighth native Virginian president, proclaimed neutrality and most citizens hoped that the United States could remain out of the conflict. The war seemed closer in 1915 when two German sea raiders, the *Prinz Eitel Friederich* and *Kron Prinz Wilhelm*, and their crews were interned at the Navy Yard. Accustomed to newspaper accounts of German destruction of Belgian villages, Portsmouth people were surprised that the internees spent their enforced leisure building a model of a peaceful German village.

After a message from President Wilson branding the German submarine policy a "warfare against mankind," Congress declared war on April 6, 1917. In that year Portsmouth's population surged to an estimated 51,000 and in 1918 reached 57,000. The Navy Yard employed 11,234 people, roughly equal to the total population of Portsmouth in the 128th year of its existence. The planned neighborhoods of Cradock and Truxton were built to house the influx of federal workers.

The Grimes Battery, one of the most venerable of such military units in the United States, and other Portsmouth National Guard organizations, shipped overseas as part of the Twenty-ninth Division. That division bore the brunt of the attack with which Gen. John J. Pershing broke "a pivotal point of the entire German system of fortifications" in the Meuse-Argonne offensive. As in other American communities, volunteers flocked to the colors. Marchers, ranging from fully uniformed sailors to business-suited men in soldier hats and puttees, became a familiar sight on Portsmouth streets.

Once again the Navy Yard had a chance to make world history. As in the case of the *Merrimac*, it did so by transforming an existing vessel into something new and launching it under another name. The job was not complete when World War I ended in 1918, but the Navy Yard converted the collier *Jupiter* into the USS *Langley*, the nation's first aircraft carrier.

The war had left, as war always does, a legacy of pain and suffering. For some, the war's end brought relief and thankfulness rather than jubilation. But, at however fearful a price, the war had left a positive legacy as well. An important element was a sense of camaraderie in separate cities and towns as well as in the great national community. Among the beneficiaries were women. The manpower shortages of the war had caused women to be recruited for jobs from which they had been turned away in earlier times. They would not again so easily be relegated to "proper work for women."

Another legacy of the war was the erection, on the site of the Jamestown Exposition and on an adjacent tract, of the greatest naval base in the western hemisphere. The building and operation of the Norfolk Naval Base increased the prosperity of all of South Hampton Roads. Work on the project began in 1917 and the new facility was commissioned for use on October 12, 1918, scarcely a month before the Armistice.

During the war, the Navy Yard in Portsmouth had gained three new drydocks capable of handling the largest battleships. The Navy Department called it "the most complicated piece of mass concrete construction ever built in this country."

During the war, also, the Portsmouth Naval Hospital had become the largest naval hospital on the East Coast.

The facilities of Portsmouth and Norfolk at the end of World War I gave Hampton Roads a concentration of naval power unrivaled in the Americas.

■

This house is in Truxton, another planned neighborhood begun during World War I to house shipyard workers. It was named for Capt. Thomas Truxton (1775-1822), credited with setting high standards of discipline and efficiency for the United States Navy.
Photo from the Rodgers Collection, courtesy Portsmouth Public Library

Rear Adm. Sir Christopher George Francis Maurice Cradock (1862-1914), was a heroic British naval officer who went down with his ship in a battle with a German squadron under Adm. Graf Spee. The planned neighborhood of Cradock, built to house the World War I influx of Navy Yard workers, was named in his honor.
Photo courtesy Portsmouth Public Library

World War I required new construction at the Navy Yard as heavier demands were placed on the local facility. Ironically, as the presence of a white horse near the center of this 1917 picture testifies, Dobbin was still important in heavy building, even when the project was a machine shop utilizing the latest technology.
U.S. Navy photo

The Grimes Battery leaves Portsmouth by railroad June 24, 1916, for duty in Mexico. Gen. John J. Pershing was leading a punitive expedition against Pancho Villa. Later the Grimes Battery shipped overseas as a part of the Twenty-ninth Division under Pershing.
Photo from the Murdaugh Collection, courtesy Portsmouth Public Library

Paradise Creek near the Navy Yard presented a scene of idyllic beauty in 1914. "Progress" covered and paved it.
Photo courtesy Portsmouth Public Library

General Neville's birthplace at First and Randolph streets is shown in a 1952 photograph.
Photo courtesy Portsmouth Public Library

This cover page of the program for unveiling and dedicating the Portsmouth Light Artillery (Grimes Battery) Monument on June 8, 1906, shows some of the people connected with the unit's proud traditions.
Program courtesy Portsmouth Public Library

Moved from its original location in the center of the street at South and Washington, the Grimes Battery monument stands today in Portsmouth City Park.
Ramona H. Mapp photo

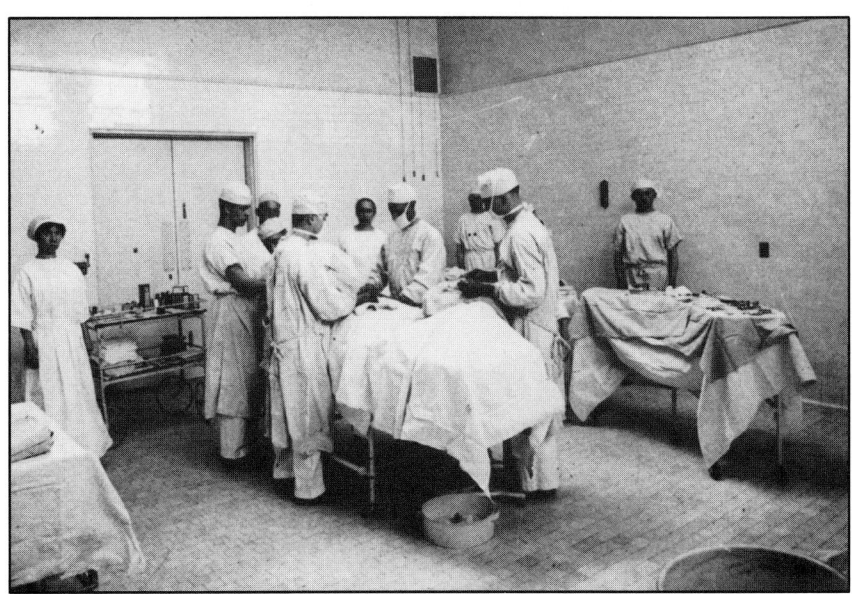

Portsmouth Naval Hospital during World War I became the largest naval hospital on the East Coast. Natural light illuminated the operating room through a dome added to the original structure in the 1907-1909 renovation.
Photo, 1917, courtesy Capt. T. H. Conaway, Naval Hospital Historian

Members of the Moonyah Club look unwontedly serious in this 1916 photo. From left to right, they are C. O. Wyatt, H. F. Watts, Tony Niemeyer, Ed. Williams, William Oast, George Larkin, J. A. Murdaugh, club president Niemeyer, Floyd French, Alex Hatton, and W. C. Niemeyer. The photo was snapped with a string under J. A. Murdaugh's foot. Photo courtesy Portsmouth Public Library

USS Langley, the nation's first Aircraft carrier, produced through conversion of the collier Jupiter at Portsmouth's Navy Yard. Photo courtesy Portsmouth Naval Shipyard Museum

Portsmouth Infantry marches south on Court Street past Trinity Episcopal Church in 1917. Most are dressed completely in civilian clothes but one can spot a military hat or two and several pairs of puttees.
Photo from the Murdaugh Collection, courtesy Portsmouth Public Library

A more martial looking group, also in 1917, marches north up Washington Street to North Street.
Photo from the Murdaugh Collection, courtesy Portsmouth Public Library

hospitals of former days

Portsmouth is served by the Naval Hospital, a still expanding giant that is already the largest Naval facility of its kind in the United States, and by two modern civilian hospitals, Portsmouth General and Maryview. In former times the city was served by much smaller institutions that deserve to be remembered.

Portsmouth's first King's Daughters Hospital, at 49 Court Street, was nurtured by the Daughters of the King, ladies' auxiliary of Trinity Episcopal Church, and took its name from that fact. The second King's Daughters Hospital, shown here, at 824 Emmett Street, was the residence of Dr. William Schmoele, purchased from him for $9,750 on January 17, 1903, as he prepared to move into his new home on Naval Place.
J. H. Downing photo, courtesy Portsmouth Public Library

Two nurses talk by the fence outside Portsmouth General's old School of Nursing.
Photo courtesy Portsmouth Public Library

In the 1950s, King's Daughters Hospital was at Fort Lane. The name was changed to Portsmouth General Hospital before its expansion in the 1960s following slum clearance in the adjacent Lincolnsville area.
Photo courtesy Portsmouth Public Library

Maryview Hospital, in the 1950s, was only the small core of the institution that sprawls today on the north side of High Street on the edge of Waterview.
Photo courtesy Portsmouth Public Library

Parrish Memorial Hospital (second building from right, with fire escape), on Court Street, began life in 1906 as the Waverly Apartments, the city's first apartment house. It was built by L. B. Watley in the expectation, richly justified, that the city would experience a large population increase as a result of the Jamestown Exposition, scheduled for the following year. After it ceased to be a hospital, the building became the Harbor Court Hotel.
Photo courtesy Portsmouth Public Library

*Fog sometimes invested the harbor with a mysterious beauty. It could also cause amusing mishaps, as on a morning in the 1940s when a Norfolk-bound ferry left its Portsmouth slip and, after following a circuitous path through the dense atmosphere, carried its passengers to the Isaac Fass docks on the Portsmouth side. Those docks and several fishing vessels are visible to the right in this outstanding 1930s photograph by Portsmouth historian J. Cloyd Emmerson.
Photo courtesy Portsmouth Public Library*

chapter eleven
UNEASY PEACE

Though Portsmouth retained much of the wartime expansion of its Navy Yard and of related businesses, it was inevitable that peace should bring a decrease in employment from the wartime peak. Many workers who had migrated to Portsmouth for defense jobs returned to their former homes. But the 1920 federal census showed Portsmouth's population as 54,387, only 2,713 less than the 1918 estimate of 57,000 when the city had seemed to be bursting at its seams. The reason was that in 1919 it had annexed the 3.4 square miles of Port Norfolk, an area substantially larger than itself although not so densely populated. This annexation also added considerably to Portsmouth's scenic waterfront. Earlier the area had been a playground for the city, providing a bathing beach, rowboats for hire, even a wharf with a restaurant and cabaret style entertainment. Balloon ascensions had been promoted by real estate firms. A principal street in Port Norfolk bore (and still bears) the name Chautauqua because the streetcar tracks that traversed its length had carried people from downtown Portsmouth to the chautauquas, the educational entertainments that had brought to the suburb some of America's most famous lecturers and musicians.

The decade of the twenties began with a national recession marked by a dramatic drop in the export trade, a matter of great importance to the cities of Hampton Roads. In 1921 no fewer than 4,750,000 Americans were unemployed.

Though the depression in agriculture remained, other aspects of the economy improved after 1921 and people were soon hailing a new era of prosperity.

In 1926 Harry Flood Byrd was elected governor of Virginia. Now remembered chiefly as a conservative United States senator, he then was hailed nationally as a remarkably progressive state executive. Like the other states of the old Confederacy, Virginia as a whole had never recovered economically from the Civil War, and its schools, other public institutions, and roads suffered as a consequence. Byrd dramatically reorganized the state government to achieve greater efficiency and won much greater appropriations for public facilities. In 1927, aided greatly by the United Daughters of the Confederacy and other Virginia organizations, he obtained nearly unanimous passage of the strongest anti-lynch law that had ever been passed by a state. It prevented the formation of lynch mobs by providing that any person present at a lynching who did not attempt to interfere was as guilty of murder as the person who placed the noose around the victim's neck. Since its passage there have been no lynchings in Virginia. The Ku Klux Klan had never been especially active in Virginia—certainly never as powerful as at various times in Mississippi, Kansas, and Maine—but passage of the Byrd Anti-lynch Law further discouraged that organiztion in the Old Dominion.

Proof of Byrd's sound management of the Commonwealth's finances lay in the fact that, whereas the state treasury had a deficit of $1,386,000 when he took office, he was able to dramatically increase spending for public services and yet leave a surplus of $4,250,000 for his successor.

The governor's campaign to "get Virginia out of the mud" had highly visible results. Portsmouth residents, for example, found many other Virginia cities far more accessible for both business and pleasure. Thanks to the state's increasing share in national prosperity, Virginians had more money than before for automobiles and motor trips. By 1929 there were 387,205 automobiles in the state and some imaginative statistician figured that, riding six to a car, all the people in the Old Dominion could be put on wheels at the same time.

Portsmouth people, no more naive than other Americans in 1929, rejoiced when a parade of economists and corporate leaders appearing before congressional committees said that the economy was sound and continued prosperity was assured. A shock wave passed through the nation on October 24 when the stock market took a historic plunge. Other dramatic drops followed, including the great one of October 29, until by November 13, $30 billion in the market value of listed stocks had been wiped out and Wall Street was in a panic.

In 1930, for the first time since the beginning of the federal decennial census in 1790, Portsmouth registered a decrease in population. The new figure was 45,704, a loss of 8,683.

People were forced to recognize that the Wall Street panic had signaled the start of a worldwide depression whose end was not in sight. Portsmouth businesses failed, jobs were lost, and continuing paychecks were reduced. But in the thirties the city was better off than most others in the United States. Modernization of two battleships, the *Mississippi* and the *Idaho*, proceeded in the Navy Yard at a cost of $12,000,000 each. Other repair work in the Yard also provided jobs. For those not fortunate enough to find steady employment, the Salvation Army and various missions furnished food and clothing.

The Depression deepened nationally between the election of Franklin D. Roosevelt as president on November 8, 1932, and his inauguration on March 4, 1933. In his inaugural address Roosevelt made his famous declaration that "the only thing we have to fear is fear itself." In ensuing days and months, he addressed the nation's fears at least as much as he did its economic problems. The country's morale improved greatly.

As Roosevelt's first term neared its end in 1937, some were alarmed at the growth of central power in his administration, but the vast majority looked to him with hope. In the contest for re-election he carried every state in the Union except Maine and Vermont. Portsmouth was one of his strongest centers of support in Virginia.

The lobby of the Hotel Monroe (formerly the Ocean House) in 1920 was complete with balcony, palms, dark paneling, and brass cuspidor.
Photo courtesy Portsmouth Public Library

The Hotel Monroe at High and Court streets is seen here in 1938. Photo courtesy Portsmouth Public Library

*A Port Norfolk Electric Railway Company car is of the sort that carried people from downtown Portsmouth to the beaches, chautauquas, and other attractions of Port Norfolk even before annexation of the suburb in 1919.
Photo courtesy Portsmouth Public Library*

*This view of High Street at Crawford was taken looking west in 1920.
Photo courtesy Portsmouth Public Library*

The New Kirn Building, built by Churchland planter and financier Henry Kirn (see group picture on page 124), provided offices for some of Portsmouth's most prominent professional people in the 1920s and later. The structure conveniently adjoined the Town Hall, with its illuminated clock above and its fire engine space below.
Photo, 1948, courtesy Portsmouth Public Library

Four means of transportation available in Portsmouth in the 1920s and 1930s appear in this postcard: bus, streetcar, automobile, and ferry (symbolized by the ferry building at the far end of High Street).
Postcard photo courtesy Everett Harrison

The persistence of an old mode of street transportation is evidenced in a somewhat later High Street scene. Besides the streetcar headed for Pinners Point, the bus behind it, and the automobiles, there are two horse-drawn wagons. Note the appearance of illuminated business signs.
Photo courtesy Portsmouth Public Library

151

Kate Smith, then America's most popular singer, performs over the Columbia Broadcasting System on October 15, 1933, at a farewell party for Adm. Richard E. Byrd on the eve of his departure from Portsmouth on his historic Antarctic expedition. Virginia's Governor John Garland Pollard sits to the left. A cold and fever kept Byrd from the festivities in Building 167 at the Navy Yard.
Photo courtesy Sargeant Memorial Room, Kirn Memorial Library

Two workers in white jackets, standing in front of a South Street cafe, enjoy the morning sunshine of March 11, 1922, after the passing of a shower that left water in the gutters, and puddles between the street railway tracks. The cornices of the cafe and of "G. Weinberg, Inc.: Lockers/Naval Outfitters" show traces of former elegance. Between the two establishments are two barbershops with striped poles. At the end of the street as seen in this picture, but in reality on the northwest corner of South and Crawford streets, is the castellated tower of the Armory and City Market.
Photo courtesy Portsmouth Public Library

Caissons and carriages pass the intersection of Middle and North streets in a 1922 Memorial Day Parade.
Photo courtesy Portsmouth Public Library

Norman R. Hamilton (1877-1964), publisher of the Portsmouth Star, *was elected to Congress for the 1937-1939 term. He was a Democrat and a supporter of President Franklin D. Roosevelt.
Photo courtesy Dick and Donna Wood*

*An unusually low tide in February 1928 uncovered debris and left this jumble of boats at the north end of Middle Street within sight of handsome residences.
From the Murdaugh collection, courtesy Portsmouth Public Library*

*The Right Reverend William Ambrose Brown (1878-1965), after serving as rector of St. John's Episcopal Church for thirty-four years, was elected bishop of the Diocese of Southern Virginia in 1938. Scholarly, eloquent, and quick-witted, the bishop was a man of commanding presence. Because Jamestown, Williamsburg, and Yorktown lay within his diocese, he often participated in commemorative programs with national and international leaders. Nevertheless, it was often said that he was the most imposing personage on the platform. His loyalty to Portsmouth was complete and fervent.
Picture courtesy Mary Brown Channel*

police and fire departments

With obvious pride, two Portsmouth policemen pose about 1914 with a police emergency car and ambulance whose gleaming hood reflects care. The little boy at right seems lost in wonder.
Photo courtesy Portsmouth Public Library

John Hunt, in 1952 one of the few surviving members of Chambers Fire Company No. 2, stands by the company's old parade reel. To the left is a ladder truck of much more recent vintage. The Chambers Hook and Ladder Company was organized in 1858 and reorganized as Chambers Engine Company No. 2 in 1866. It was one of at least eight volunteer fire companies organized in Portsmouth, beginning with the Resolution Fire Company in 1830. This parade reel, topped by a symbolic greyhound, was built about 1870 and was pulled by hand in torchlight processions. The various volunteer companies were rivals not only in swift response to emergency calls but also in spiffy appearance on parade.
Photo courtesy Portsmouth Public Library

Portsmouth's entire Police Department assembled at the entrance to police headquarters for this group portrait about 1905. Second from the right in the second row is J. M. Broughton, later the only man to have the distinction of serving as both police chief and fire chief of the city. After his retirement, Chief Broughton was for many years honorary president of the International Association of Police Chiefs. Shown from left to right are (front row) William Diggs, Lt. C. L. Cadmus, Lewis Calvert, William Andarton, Chief F. T. Tynan, and Asst. Chief A. H. Onley; (second row) John Taylor, Harry C. Hall, Jessie Diggs, William Land, William Dillsburg, J. M. Broughton, and D. P. Culpepper. The three men in the third row are unidentified. The boy at the top was the son of the jailer at the Norfolk County jail. Photo courtesy Portsmouth Public Library

In this photo, taken about 1915, the Police Department has doubled in size and its members wear a different style of hats but the same serious demeanor. Photo courtesy Portsmouth City Police Department

Three vehicles line up at the Cradock Fire Station for an early photo. Photo courtesy Portsmouth Public Library

Three vehicles of the Navy Yard Fire Department, suggesting Papa Bear, Mama Bear, and Baby Bear, go on display on May 6, 1920.
U.S. Navy photo,
courtesy Portsmough Public Library

Fire Chief W. B. Sykes (left) and S. Deale Blanchard (second from right) president of the Portsmouth Junior Chamber of Commerce, dedicate a monument in 1946 on the grounds of Fire Headquarters at 361 Effingham Street. The inscription reads "In tribute [to] original Grant multiversal nozzle invented by Jordan Winslow Grant, master mechanic 1923-1937, Portsmouth Fire Department." An example of the invention surmounts the monument erected by Portsmouth Jaycees. Standing next to Sykes is Sherwood Brockwell, fire marshal for the State of North Carolina. At far right is David M. Grant, nephew of the inventor.
Photo courtesy Portsmouth Public Library

Members of Chambers Fire Company No. 2, clad in traditional helmets and pulling a small signal or salute cannon, march north up Washington Street in 1917.
From the Murdaugh Collection, courtesy Portsmouth Public Library

Promoting Fire Safety Week, a Fire Department vehicle is parked in the first block of High Street in front of the old Portsmouth Star building. Such vehicles, though among the best of their time, are a far cry from the sophisticated equipment now used by the Fire Department under the direction of Odell Benton, chief since 1953. The favorable fire insurance ratings granted the city of Portsmouth testify to the department's efficiency.
Photo courtesy Portsmouth Public Library

Sailors, most in summer whites, are prominent in this World War II photo looking west up High Street from the ferries. The Portsmouth Star *building is on the left. The ferry docks, a Greyhound bus terminal, the Victory Navy Store, A & N Stores, a Western Union office, and nearby theaters made this block attractive to sailors.*
Photo courtesy Portsmouth Public Library

chapter twelve
WORLD WAR II

Though Roosevelt continued to fight economic troubles energetically and imaginatively and succeeded in alleviating them, the nation was still in the Depression when a shocking event solved that long-standing problem by presenting the United States with an even greater one. On Sunday, December 7, 1941, the Japanese attacked the United States Naval Base at Pearl Harbor, Hawaii, sinking or disabling nineteen ships. The report of the attack was received at 1:20 p.m. Portsmouth time. Many people in the city had returned from church and were enjoying Sunday dinner or relaxing afterwards when the shocking news interrupted the music from their radios.

No one would have asked for so painful a solution to the Depression, but Roosevelt himself said that the nation's sick economy was cured by "Dr. Win-the-War."

No community in the United States made a greater contribution to victory over the Axis Powers than Hampton Roads, and the work of Portsmouth's Navy Yard was an indispensable part of that contribution. Soon shipyard workers were pouring into Portsmouth from other parts of Virginia, and in especially large numbers from North Carolina, West Virginia, and Kentucky. Virtually every state was represented in the influx that boosted shipyard employment to 43,000. At least 16,437 housing units were built in Portsmouth and neighboring cities specifically to accommodate shipyard workers, and Cradock experienced a boom reminiscent of its birth in World War I. Buses were overloaded and people stood in line for almost everything. But most people thought a little inconvenience was a small price to pay for victory, particularly in view of the sacrifices of friends and relatives in uniform. Beginning in 1942, people followed the fortunes of local soldier, sailors, marines, and Air Force personnel, as well as of ships built or repaired in the Navy Yard, through the newscasts of Portsmouth's first radio station, WSAP. The facility was the ancestor of the later WAVY radio and present WAVY-TV.

The most shocking public news came April 12, 1945, in the announcement that President Franklin D. Roosevelt had died of a massive cerebral hemorrhage. The city greatly admired the wartime chief whose policies had done so much for the navy town and whose warm personality had won friends on a visit to the Navy Yard. In few communities was he mourned more greatly than here.

The recent death of the president and the continuing struggle with Japan lent a note of sobriety to the celebration of V-E Day, May 8, 1945, marking victory in Europe.

V-J Day, August 15, 1945, marking the end of the war with Japan, saw thousands of celebrants pour into the streets of downtown Portsmouth. At the intersection of Court and High streets, sailor caps, like whitecaps on the ocean, danced on a sea of humanity. Strangers, civilian and military, embraced. Only the stone sailors and soldiers on the intersection's central monument remained unmoved.

Portsmouth could be proud of its contributions. Its citizens had served on every front, almost always with credit, sometimes with distinction. From January 1940 to the end of the war with Japan the Navy Yard had constructed 101 new ships and landing craft and had worked on 6,850 warships of the United States and its allies.

*Trailer camps sprouted to house the influx of Navy Yard workers.
Photo courtesy Portsmouth Public Library*

*Workers wait for a bus at the Navy Yard's Fourth Street Gate in 1944. The city's public transportation was severely burdened.
Photo courtesy Portsmouth Public Library*

*A defense worker and his family, drawn from North Carolina by the increase in Navy Yard employment even before United States entry into World War II, make a neat home of their one-room apartment in Portsmouth in March 1941.
Photo courtesy the Chrysler Museum, Norfolk, Va.*

*Rising employment did not solve the financial problems of all. At the Helping Hand Mission an elderly woman takes up a collection for the needy while others sing a hymn, in March 1941.
Photo courtesy the Chrysler Museum, Norfolk, Va.*

first citizens of portsmouth

Some Portsmouth First Citizens have almost as many years as honors when they receive the award, first presented in 1932, and then under the aegis of the Loyal Order of Moose in every year since 1939. But some have been surprisingly youthful, as was Judge Lawrence W. I'Anson (center) in 1946 when he received it from his immediate predecessor, T. A. Willett (right). The judge later became Chief Justice of Virginia.
Photo courtesy Portsmouth Public Library

*Norman R. Hamilton	1932
*John A. Morris	1939
*Edward W. Maupin, Jr.	1940
*Rt. Rev. Msgr. F. Harold Nott	1941
*Frank D. Lawrence	1942
*Rear Admiral Felix X. Gygax	1943
*George T. McLean	1944
*T. A. Willett	1945
Chief Justice Lawrence W. I'Anson	1946
*Leslie T. Fox	1947
*Sol Fass	1948
*Maywood O. Lawrence	1949
*Abner B. Hill	1950
Hon. Porter Hardy, Jr.	1951
Lewis C. Warren	1952
Rev. Ernest K. Emurian	1953
*J. Roy Rodman	1954
*O. B. Woolridge	1955
*Harry A. Hunt	1956
*Rt. Rev. William A. Brown	1957
*Prof. A. J. Lancaster	1958
*Fred Beazley	1959
Arthur Lee Cherry	1960
Richard F. Wood	1961
*Dr. Russell Mills Cox	1962
*George T. Ewell	1963
*Lester Lloyd Knight	1964
*John Tydings Nix	1965
Wilfred F. Magann	1966
Dr. Robert Monroe Campbell	1967
Judge John Ashton MacKenzie	1968
Edwin Saunders Early, Jr.	1969
Robert Murdaugh Reed	1970
*Dr. Merl A. Kise	1971
Paul Curtis Stokely	1972
Hon. Richard J. Davis	1973
Herbert K. Bangel	1974
P. Stockton Fleming	1975
*Emily Nichols Spong	1976
Frank Langley Kirby	1977
George Delman Eastes	1978
Daniel W. Duncan	1979
Robert William Wentz, Jr.	1980
Rear Admiral Jamie Adair, USN, Ret.	1981
Emile S. Sayegh, M. D.	1982
Peter Eustis	1983
Bradford L. Cherry	1984
John Paul Conwell Hanbury	1985
J. Herbert Simpson	1986
Anne Hyde Long	1987

*Indicates deceased citizens

HMS Illustrious, *a British aircraft carrier, entered the Navy Yard for repairs May 12, 1941, after extensive damage off Malta in a German dive bomber attack. Before the departure of the ship November 25, 1941, it welcomed aboard its recently appointed captain, Lord Louis Mountbatten, great-grandson of Queen Victoria and cousin to King George V. During the ship's stay in Portsmouth, it was visited by the Duke of Kent, the king's brother. Mountbatten two years later was named Supreme Allied Commander, Southeast Asia, and was later viceroy and governor general of India and first lord of the admiralty. At the time Portsmouth people thought that the Duke of Kent was the most interesting royal visitor to the city since the reception and ball for the Russian Grand dukes Alexis and Constantine in 1877 and that the handsome, forty-one-year-old Mountbatten was the most glamorous foreign officer welcomed to Portsmouth since the Marquis de Lafayette. The Illustrious was one of six British naval ships repaired in the Yard in 1941 before United States entry into World War II. As a token of friendship, workers at the facility presented to the* Illustrious *a new ship's bell to replace a damaged one.*
Photo courtesy Portsmouth
Public Library

Mrs. James H. Doolittle, wife of the general who led the April 18, 1942, carrier-based raid on Tokyo, prepares to christen the aircraft carrier Shangri-La *at the Navy Yard in 1944. When the Japanese wondered where American warplanes had come from, President Roosevelt said "Shangri-La" in playful allusion to the mythical land in James Hilton's novel* Lost Horizon. *Taking him literally, the Japanese government announced that the American attack had been launched from a carrier called Shangri-La. Roosevelt then suggested that a United States carrier be given the name.*
Photo courtesy Portsmouth
Public Library

President Franklin D. Roosevelt, holding his panama hat to his chest in salute, visits the Navy Yard. Standing in public was always painful for the polio-crippled Chief Executive. The wartime leader was extremely popular in Portsmouth.
Photo courtesy Portsmouth
Public Library

Mrs. Bertha Winborne Edwards became Portsmouth's first black librarian when the Portsmouth Community Library opened December 20, 1945. Among the most valuable artifacts saved by Mrs. Edwards are those of Lee Rodgers.
Photo courtesy of Mrs. Bertha Winborne Edwards

Chamber of Commerce Executive Secretary Ray J. Dunn, hat in hand, prepares to take off in a craft bearing the name of the Portsmouth Chamber of Commerce. His mission was to present a plan for building the United Nations headquarters on Craney Island. City Engineer Bergeron (standing on ground), sees him off.
Photo courtesy Portsmouth Public Library

Lee F. Rodgers, far left, Portsmouth Star columnist and "Colored Notes" editor in the segregated days of the 1930s and 1940s, was frequently not only the chronicler but the instigator of moves for black economic and cultural advancement in Portsmouth. He was a consummate diplomat and an accomplished raconteur. His collection of papers and pictures, in the Portsmouth Public Library, is a rich trove for historians of the city.
Photo from the Rodgers Collection, courtesy Portsmouth Public Library

trains

While the romance of the sea has always captured the hearts of Portsmouth youngsters, the whistles of trains have sometimes competed with those of boats as siren calls. Especially was this true in the age of the steam locomotive, a great wailing beast snorting a plume of billowing smoke. Many railroad engineers lived in Portsmouth, and their sons and daughters were often the envy of schoolmates. Some of these gods of the throttle played favorite tunes on their train whistles or used them to send coded messages to their famlies. Many young boys—and some girls—longed to become engineers. Even those who didn't dreamed of adventures in far places as, lying in bed, they heard a long-drawn whistle fade out in the distant night.

This locomotive and coal car, marked with the initials of the Savannah, Americus & Montgomery Railway, began serving the Seaboard in 1900. Baldwin-Broadbelt photo

Two Seaboard Coast Line locomotives wait at the railroad's Portsmouth shops in a 1976 snowstorm. Hugh Griffin, Jr. photo, courtesy Portsmouth Public Library

A Belt Line engine, caboose, and freight cars cross a bridge on a misty day. Naval Shipyard photo, courtesy Portsmouth Public Library

Seaboard Engine No. 16 travels down the track under a dark plume of smoke.
Photo courtesy Portsmouth Public Library

The Seaboard Building is shown sometime after the 1906 fire. Two more stories were added later.
Photo courtesy Portsmouth Public Library

In 1962 this Seaboard Air Line Railway freight office, said to have been the first in Portsmouth, was a deteriorating relic.
Photo from the Murdaugh Collection, courtesy Portsmouth Public Library

A crew of four stands beside a Seaboard engine in this undated photo.
Photo courtesy Portsmouth Public Library

Pinners Point Railroad Yards in 1959. On the left are tracks of the Southern and of the Atlantic and Danville. On the right are those of the Atlantic Coast Line. In 1970 this would be the location of "the world's first completely planned cargo port."
Photo courtesy Portsmouth Public Library

A Seaboard shifter works the Crawford Street tracks in 1958.
Photo courtesy Portsmouth Public Library

People wait in line to board the Freedom Train, visiting Portsmouth afer World War II with a collection of documents and mementoes of American history. Note the Marine guard near the center of the picture.
Photo courtesy Portsmouth Public Library

A Seaboard Air Line Railroad porter holds a gift-wrapped package and reads a card while a fellow porter watches his expression with pleasure and anticipation. This January 1958 photo probably shows a scene from a retirement party. Maybe some reader will recognize the participants. The Seaboard had its beginnings in Portsmouth in 1832 as the Portsmouth and Roanoke Railroad Company, was reorganized in 1846 as the Seaboard and Roanoke Railroad, and finally became the Seaboard Air Line. The removal of its corporate headquarters to Richmond, on August 22, 1958, was a sad day for many workers and their friends as well as for all concerned about the city's economic health.
Photo courtesy Portsmouth Public Library

The Seaboard gave its 1894 passenger station to the city for use as a municipal building. In June 1970, city offices moved from the old building to the new Civic Center. There was talk of tearing down the structure, but in January 1988 it became the home of apartments, offices, and The Max, a glittering Art Deco restaurant with a magnificent view of the harbor. Once marked for destruction, the building was saved through efforts led by Mrs. Emily Spong.
Jim Hall photo

Mayor Jack Barnes, flanked by Graham Claytor, president of the Southern Railroad, and John (Jack) Nix, assistant director of the Virginia Port Authority, drives the last spike in the track linking the railroad with Portsmouth International Terminals.
Photo courtesy Jack P. Barnes

sports

It is appropriate that Portsmouth is the home of the Virginia Sports Hall of Fame, founded in 1971 under the leadership of J. Herbert Simpson, because surely no Virginia community has produced more sports champions per capita than this city.

National attention is drawn each year by the Ladies' Professional Golf Association Tournament at Portsmouth's Sleepy Hole Golf Course. The event is sponsored by CRESTAR, formerly United Virginia Bank, with the aid of the Portsmouth Service League. In May 1988 the ninth annual tournament's $250,000 purse attracted a field of 142 L.P.G.A. players and two amateurs. About thirty thousand spectators—an all-time high—attended the four-day event and the Service League earned $32,000 for its charitable projects.

Chandler Harper, one of the world's great golfers, was elected to the Professional Golfers' Hall of Fame in 1969. For other information, see "Portsmouth's National Notables."
Photo courtesy Portsmouth Public Library

The Portsmouth Juniors Football Team of 1901 was a group of young athletes not associated with any school. This team played others in the Portsmouth and Norfolk area and was undefeated for four successive seasons. Members are, left to right, (first row) Johnson Neely, Bilisoly Hudgins, and E. L. "Buck" Baker; (second row) Hinton Craft, Homer Wample, Billie Bruce, and Tom Hume; (third row) Beany Trant (manager), Jimmie Hume, George Bacot, Dinks Marshall, Collins Hill, and Lee Watts (assistant manager).
Photo courtesy Barnabas W. "Billy" Baker

Robert G. Rowland was named to the Marine Racing Hall of Fame in 1951, the same year that he set a five-mile world's record and was chosen outstanding driver in the United States.
Photo courtesy Portsmouth Public Library

Jean McLean (center), winner of more equestrienne awards than any other American woman, is honored at a banquet in her hometown. She is flanked (left, partially behind trophy) by her father, George T. McLean, one of the most successful industrialists in Portsmouth history, and Ray J. Dunn, then executive secretary of the Portsmouth Chamber of Commerce. To the right is Mrs. McLean. The stable of horses on the family's Churchland estate included several world champions, among them Oak Hill Chief, for five successive years the world's champion five-gaited horse. Note the gleaming trophies and array of ribbons in the foreground. The broadcast call letters WSAP were those of the present WAVY.
Photo courtesy Portsmouth Public Library

Clarence "Ace" Parker was once called "the world's greatest football player." Elected to the College Football Hall of Fame in 1955, the Virginia Sports Hall of Fame in 1972, and Football Hall of Fame in 1977, he was a remarkably versatile athlete, in his Wilson High School days excelling in golf, baseball, and track. For other information, see "Portsmouth's National Notables."
Photo courtesy Portsmouth Public Library

Junius Kellogg is celebrated not only as a great basketball player but also as a courageous man who uncovered corruption in the sport. For other information, see "Portsmouth's National Notables." Photo from the Rodgers Collection, courtesy Portsmouth Public Library

Doris S. Leigh makes another strike. In 1969 she was elected to the National Duckpin Bowling Hall of Fame. Photo courtesy Portsmouth Public Library

*Ferries are in two of the four slips at the foot of High Street and the small ferry Berkley is headed for its dock in this 1950s (?) photo. The Seaboard Building is to the left near a ferry slip. The near-white steeple of the First Presbyterian Church, on Court Street, rises in the left background. Just a little to the right of the steeple are the old Town Hall cupola with the town clock and the four-square tower of Trinity Episcopal Church. The six lanes of High Street sweep grandly westward to the horizon. On the north (or right) side of the street, the pinnacle of its steeple at the top of the picture, is St. Paul's Catholic Church. To the right and slightly nearer the viewer is Monumental Methodist Church.
Photo courtesy Fifth Coast Guard District*

chapter thirteen
MIXED SIGNALS

As the pace of work in the shipyard eased to a peacetime level, many warworkers returned to their earlier homes elsewhere in Virginia and in other states. But Portsmouth grew again in 1948 by annexation of two Norfolk County communities, Westhaven and Waterview. The move increased the city's area from 5.8 square miles to 9.7. The federal 1950 federal census showed a population of 80,039, a gain of 29,294 over the 1940 figure.

By 1950 Navy Yard employment had reached its lowest level since the heights of World War II, but even so 9,025 persons were at work there, still a substantially larger number than the 7,625 employed at the outbreak of war in Europe in September 1939. The outbreak of the Korean War in June 1950 quickly reversed the trend. By August 1952 employment in the Yard reached 16,090. In August of that year Portsmouth celebrated its two hundredth birthday with a program of education and pageantry chaired by Marshall W. Butt, founder of the Naval Shipyard Museum and a faithful chronicler of the city's story.

Ironically, an event in Portsmouth's bicentennial year doomed one of its most cherished links with the past. On May 23 a newly constructed tunnel opened to vehicular traffic between Portsmouth and Norfolk. For the first time, the Elizabeth River ferries faced stiff competition. When Norfolk County, on February 16, 1954, offered to sell its half interest in them to Portsmouth and the city did not consider the investment justified, the approaching end was obvious. On August 25, 1955, the ferries made their last run. Suspension of the ferries made national news as the operation, dating from 1636, was described as the oldest of its kind in the United States.

The tunnel had both speeded and increased the flow of traffic between the two cities and the volume soon exceeded professional prognostications. The tube was recognized as indispensable to Portsmouth's economy. No one would want to give up the efficiency of the new transportation, but most felt that a lot of fun and a great deal of poetry had vanished with the ferries.

In the last days of ferry operation this writer sought in a newspaper article[1] to convey some of the romance of the old way of travel:

The harbor scene is one that fascinates most tourists in the Norfolk-Portsmouth area. They crowd out on the aprons of the ferries, rain or shine, and eagerly peer in every direction.

It is frequently hard, though, to distinguish between tourists and commuters. The man who braves gusts of rain to survey harbor activity may make the round trip every day.

The scene is not monotonous to him because it is always different.

Make the trip on a sunny day. Light sparkles on blue waves under a blue sky, and even the sea gulls seem freshly washed. Almost midway of the crossing, just opposite Hospital Point, the neo-classical dome of the Naval Hospital gleams in the sunshine.

Perhaps a trim little Navy launch will cut across the ferry's path and suddenly swerve out of the way in a manner that is positively rakish. Red tugs plow along purposefully with an air of commendable industry.

[1] Alf J. Mapp, Jr., "Norfolk County Ferries Face the Final Voyage," the *Virginian-Pilot* and the *Portsmouth Star*, August 14, 1955 Section, C, p. 1.

Sometimes a sleek gray Navy crusier will move so near the ferry that passengers can see the faces of bluejackets lining the rail.

Occasionally passengers are treated to the sight of helicopters hanging like poised dragonflies over the flight deck of an aircraft carrier.

At night, the ferry traveler between Norfolk and Portsmouth is in a different world. As the lights of Commercial Place recede, the pale green lights of the Berkley Bridge appear on the port side. On a dark night, the shadowy form of the bridge fades into the general blackness and lighted vehicles moving across the arch appear to be flying through space.

Later the giant form of the Naval Shipyard crane, decked with white and red lights as for a celebration, is seen towering above the white constellation that marks the busy Federal installation.

As the boat nears the Portsmouth docks, the long, lighted vista of Queen Street suddenly appears and abruptly disappears and one is reminded of the experience of looking out the windows of a moving train whose tracks bisect the avenues of a city.

Then come the ferry house and the dock shed. They are carnival-like in architecture, and the red, blue, green and yellow neon lights of High Street, seen through the arch, heighten the effect.

But the view from a ferry deck is not the same every night. Fog invests the harbor with mystery. Then lights glimmer faintly through the darkness, sometimes moving above the surface of the water like will-o'-the-wisps.

The whole world seems an amorphous one of sky and water, and foghorns and deep-throated boat whistles sound like primeval creatures calling to each other from the deep.

The passenger standing in the bow may be surprised to see a sea gull suddenly start from the surface of the water only a few feet away and as suddenly disappear, like some pale ghost of a bird.

Perhaps a sister vessel passes, the sound of its movement muffled by the fog, its lights glowing yellow in the night like the lanterns of Charon's ferry.

■

The year 1955 brought a change even more important to Portsmouth than loss of the ferries. In 1954 the city had initiated formal proceedings to annex about 25 square miles of Norfolk County. The city argued that the density of its population, with more than 80,000 people crowded into 9.7 square miles, cried out for relief. Its attorneys pointed out that people living to the south and west of the city's borders were enjoying Portsmouth's urban facilities while benefiting from the lower tax rates of the county. Moreover, Portsmouth's future was threatened by the beginning of a migration of the citizens to the suburbs. Fearing a series of amputations by both Portsmouth and Norfolk, Norfolk County fought hard. Though Portsmouth lost its suit on a technicality in 1955, an appeal obtained a large measure of redress. Effective January 1, 1960, the city was awarded 10 square miles, including Cradock, Alexander Park, Simonsdale, Elizabeth Manor, and other suburban neighborhoods. Portsmouth's area jumped to 18.8 square miles. Its population numbered 114,775, making it the third largest city in Virginia, ranking behind Norfolk with 304,869 and Richmond with 219,958.

More significant than Portsmouth's climb up the population ladder was the fact that the annexation gave the city room for growth and an improved tax base. The city profited from being the home of the nation's leading naval shipyard, but it suffered form the fact that so much of its real estate was owned by the federal government and therefore not subject to municipal taxation. If Portsmouth had been confined within its pre-1960 borders, it would have been doomed to decay.

Smarting from the loss of some of its best residential real estate and facing the fact that annexation left its courts and offices in Portsmouth even farther removed from most Norfolk County citizens, the county moved its seat from Portsmouth to Great Bridge. Thus ended the arrangement whereby Norfolk County's government had been centered in Portsmouth since 1803.

The county took an even more drastic step to guard against further annexation. It joined with the city of South Norfolk to create on January 1, 1963, the city of Chesapeake.

This action, however, was too late to prevent resolution in Portsmouth's favor of an annexation suit already pending. After a long-drawn court battle, Portsmouth, on January 1, 1968, gained West Norfolk, Craney Island, and much of the affluent Churchland and other Western Branch areas. The city's area expanded to thirty square miles.

In this moment of success, however, the signals for Portsmouth's future were mixed. Over the preceding decade and a half the city's fortunes had ranged up and down the economic scale, demonstrating all too clearly the city's heavy dependence on the Navy Yard. To an even greater extent than in most American cities, and with a shifting more abrupt, the economic welfare of Portsmouth depended upon decisions made in Washington, which in turn were based on decisions made in foreign captials. In 1953 Portsmouth had rejoiced that its per capita income had more than doubled in six years. The advance was real and not just a phantom progress, the product of inflation. A municipal chronicler noted that in 1947 "business in the city was nearly twice the national rate, increasing 213 percent since 1941." But in 1954, the very year after Portsmouth celebrated the doubling of per capita income, the Naval Shipyard reduced its work force, halting economic growth. In October 1959 the Yard imposed a job ceiling of eleven thousand and Portsmouth's economy went into reverse. A partial recovery began eleven months later when the Yard began work on both conventional and nuclear submarines.

Various losses and other changes during the fifties and sixties had created a climate of doubt and discouragement. In 1955 the *Portsmouth Star*, Portsmouth's only newspaper, had been sold to Norfolk Newspapers, publishers of the *Virginian-Pilot* and the *Ledger-Dispatch*. The Norfolk papers were respected and many Portsmouth people had subscribed to one of them as well as to the *Star*. Moreover, the *Star*'s name was to be incorporated into the names of the Norfolk publications. But many Portsmouth citizens felt frustration at having no newspaper published within their own borders. They suffered from a sense of colonial status. A downtown fire on August 9, 1957, had destroyed the Hotel Monroe, a landmark since its origin as the Ocean House in 1853, and had wiped out thirteen other businesses. And the Seaboard Air Line Railroad, which had been one of Portsmouth's major employers since its founding in the city in 1832 as the Portsmouth and Roanoke Railroad Company, moved its corporate headquarters to Richmond in 1958.

Optimists pointed out that removal of the Seaboard's tracks from Crawford Street permitted the return of the thoroughfare of fine old homes to prestigious residential status. They also pointed out that the city's acquisition of extensive waterfront property formerly owned by the railroad provided opportunities for both commercial development and beautification. Slum clearance began in 1960 with removal of substandard housing in the thirty-four-acre Lincolnsville area bounded by North and Washington streets, Fort Lane, and the Naval Hospital. It was certain that the city would benefit from more of such clearances, though it was apparent that some in their zeal were ready to eliminate cultural landmarks as well as blight. Some businesses were moving from downtown to shopping malls, but the downtown was provided a new anchor in 1961 when a new $3.5 million Federal Building was dedicated on Crawford Street. It not only housed the city's central post office but also, besides other federal offices, the Fifth District Coast Guard Headquarters, which moved from Norfolk. Heavy traffic between Portsmouth and Norfolk necessitated construction of a second Elizabeth River tube, the Midtown Tunnel, connecting Pinners Point in Portsmouth with Hampton Boulevard in Norfolk. Work began in April 1960 and the facility opened on September 2, 1962. And, if Portsmouth had lost its newspaper, it had gained its own television voice. WAVY-TV began its telecasts in September 1957.

Under the leadership of Mayor R. Irvine Smith, a railroad man with a keen awareness of the possibilities of rail and sail cooperation, Portsmouth determined to become "the world's first completely planned container cargo port." The city thus could capitalize on the interest of both railroads and shipping lines in "piggy-back" cargo operations that would save many man-hours in loading and unloading. The dream was realized September 20, 1967, when the Portsmouth Marine Terminal began operations at Pinners Point, giving Portsmouth an advantage over all its East Coast competitors in a revolutionary cargo-handling development.

Amid all the arguments of optimists and pessimists, there was one sobering fact that all had to acknowledge: the 1970 census revealed that Portsmouth, although its area had increased since the 1960 census from 18.8 square miles to 30, had suffered a population decrease from 110,963 to 104,577. The population decrease was only the second for the city since the institution of the federal census in 1790. It had occurred despite the fact that the United States had been engaged in the undeclared

coast guard

In 1870 the United States government purchased land at First and Randolph streets for the Lighthouse Service. The Lighthouse Service in 1939 became part of the Coast Guard and the original three-quarter-acre lot expanded to nine acres. Portsmouth became headquarters for the Fifth Coast Guard District, including Virginia, North Carolina, Maryland, and the District of Columbia.

Though the Coast Guard's link with Portsmouth does not go as far back as the Navy's, it is nevertheless an old and cherished one. It is symbolized by the Coast Guard ship Portsmouth, *now anchored in cement, which has been a popular museum and a prominent feature of the waterfront since 1967. The happy association of the city and service is also symbolized by the facts that a Portsmouth native, Rear Adm. Edward C. Allen, Jr., was commander of this Coast Guard district from 1967 to 1971, and that Rear Adm. Julian E. (Joe) Johansen, district commander from 1975 to 1978, not only remained in Portsmouth after retirement but became its mayor from 1980 to 1984.*
Photo courtesy Fifth Coast Guard District

The downtown base (above) was long outgrown when, in July 1971, Admiral Allen and United States Senator William B. Spong, Jr., broke ground for the new base at Craney Island for which they both had campaigned. The present base, shown in the 1979 photo, occupies a 187-acre site at the foot of Coast Guard Boulevard.
Photos courtesy Fifth Coast Guard District

Vietnam War, its involvement having begun under President Truman with military and economic aid to anti-Communists in the divided country and gradually increased under Eisenhower and Kennedy until it was sharply escalated in 1965 when President Johnson sent in United States combat troops and ordered bombing raids in North Vietnam.

If the dwindling of Portsmouth's population was cause for concern, some of its qualities gave reason for hope. Some communities in the United States complained that they had the pain of fighting a war on two fronts. Portsmouth was not one of them. The complaining communities referred to a domestic crisis that occurred during the deepening of United States involvement in Vietnam. In 1954 the United States Supreme Court ruled in *Brown v. Board of Education* that segregation in public education was a "denial of equal protection of the laws," and in 1955 the court directed lower courts to admit blacks to previously segregated schools "with all deliberate speed." Various states and communities acted in a variety of ways to subvert the ruling. The General Assembly of Virginia on February 1, 1956, harking back to constitutional theories of the early republic, adopted an interposition resolution asserting the right of the Commonwealth to "interpose its sovereignty" between its people and the court. Virginia political leaders joined those from some other states in calling for resistance by "all lawful means." In Virginia the policy was called "massive resistance." As a result of this policy some Virginia schools were closed, most conspicuously in Norfolk where, on Monday, September 29, 1958, all public high schools were closed, shutting out ten thousand students. Many Norfolkians, in and out of the school system, strove fruitlessly to prevent the closing.

Meanwhile, by mutual agreement among white and black leaders, Portsmouth took the first steps toward full integration of its public schools. The city's schools began with token admissions rather than resistance. The first steps were too small in the view of many blacks and too bold in the opinion of many whites. But the percentage of integration was gradually increased from year to year. No violence marred the transition. Some students denied a high school education in Norfolk obtained one in Portsmouth.

By 1959 the state, after rousing rancor by "massive resistance," adopted a policy of initiating token integration and expanding it to a significant level. Norfolk schools reopened.

Portsmouth people were proud of the orderly way in which blacks and whites had worked together. Much credit for peaceful integration was given to the mutual trust of two white officials, School Board Chairwoman Emily Spong and School Superintendent Alf J. Mapp, and two black leaders, William E. Waters, Jr., and Harvey N. Johnson, Sr. Other citizens of both races also made important contributions. Another factor was that the Superintendent, throughout his administration, had appointed able blacks to responsible administrative and supervisory positions and had worked strongly to upgrade black schools.

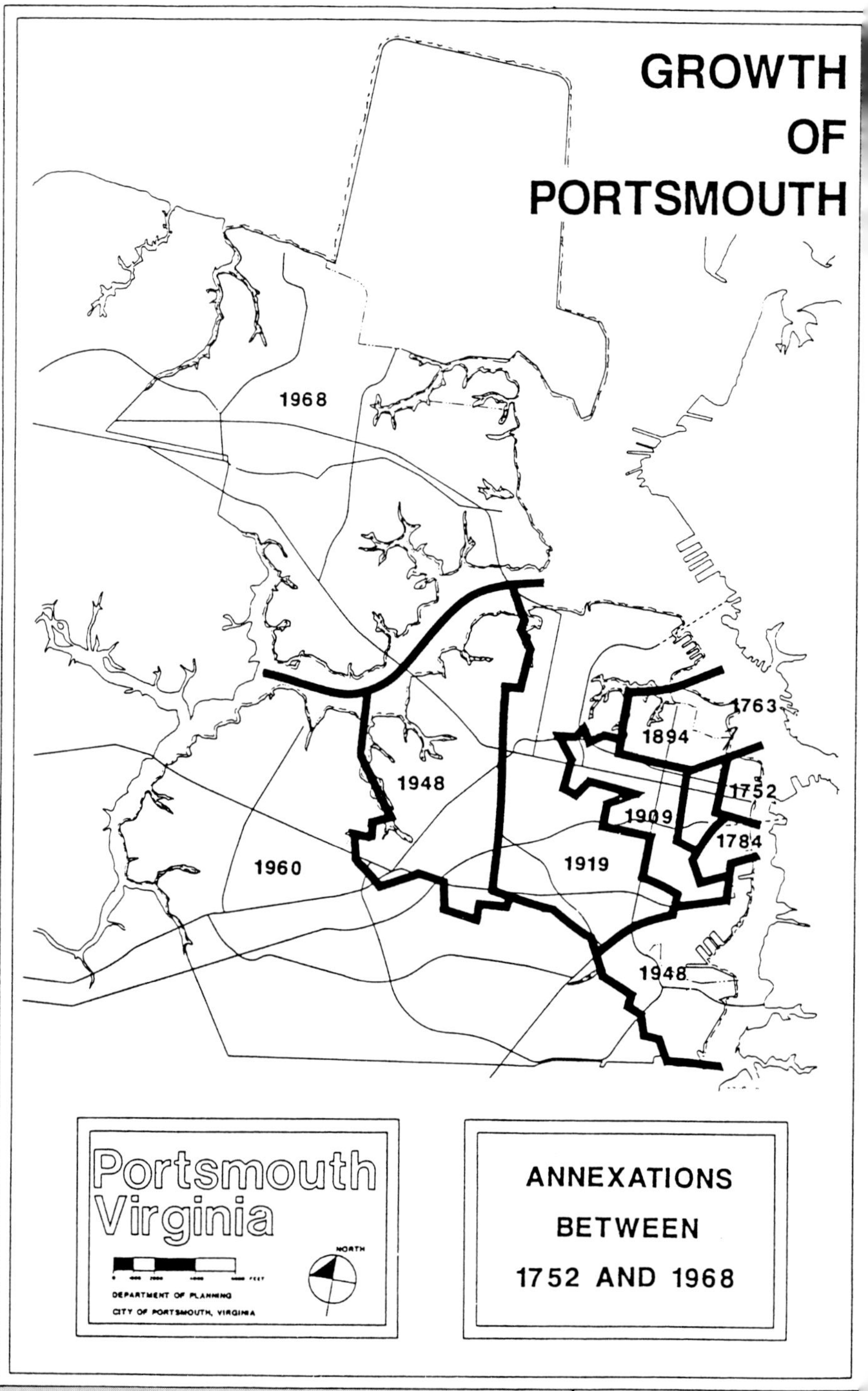

GROWTH OF PORTSMOUTH

ANNEXATIONS BETWEEN 1752 AND 1968

A portion of the downtown waterfront wears a look of romantic desuetude in this 1950 photo that has a decided turn-of-the century air. Three rowboats float in the mouth of the slip, at the foot of North Street, used by Portsmouth-Norfolk County ferries before 1839. A portion of Pier No. 9 of the Seaboard Air Line Railway is on the left. Faintly visible on the right are Piers 10 and 11.
Virginia Port Authority photo, courtesy Portsmouth Public Library

Marshall W. Butt, a Portsmouth historian with strong personal and ancestral ties to the city, was chairman in 1952 of the Portsmouth, Virginia, Bicentennial commemorating the founding of the town by Col. William Crawford. Here he stands by a model of USS Delaware in the Portsmouth Naval Shipyard Museum, which he founded in 1949 and served as first director. This photo was made before the museum moved from the Navy Yard to the foot of High Street.
Photo courtesy Portsmouth Public Library

A dormered nineteenth-century building with iron grillework balconies houses an automobile battery service and a motorcycle salesroom at 401-403 Crawford Street in 1954 as past and present reach an uneasy accommodation. The structure was among those razed in the same year to make way for the new Federal Building.
Photo courtesy Portsmouth Public Library

High Street in the 1950s would have been instantly recognizable to anyone who had seen it more than a half century earlier. The 1846 Court House was to the left behind the tree extending over the sidewalk. Beyond Court Street on the same side was the home of The Famous. Beyond is the sign of the Gates Theater. In right foreground is Trinity Episcopal Church, and across Court Street is the New Kirn Building.
Photo courtesy Portsmouth Public Library

Except for a few parked automobiles, this block on the west side of Middle Street, looking toward London Boulevard, seems deserted. Creech's Jewelers' clock, a familiar landmark, says that it is nearly two o'clock, but the shadows suggest that it is just a little past noon on this July 1, 1951. Maybe the people are eating at The Candle, a tea room which occupies the old Nash home. The Slenderizing Salon in the right forefront may have reminded some diners to practice moderation. Between The Candle and Queen Street are the O'Rourke (with awning-shaded balcony) and Brooks houses.

Photo from the Murdaugh Collection, courtesy Portsmouth Public Library

An extraordinarily valuable resource person in Portsmouth's observance of its two hundredth anniversary was J. Cloyd Emmerson, businessman, former newspaper editor, and scion of a family long prominent in the city. His compilations, like Marshall Butt's, are essential to any student of Portsmouth's past.
Photo courtesy Portsmouth Public Library

Substantial homes on tree-lined streets are visible in this aerial view of Portsmouth with Swimming Point in the foreground. In contrast, at mid-level and to the far right are the gas works, which would be removed in 1955, making way for attractive residences. On the horizon a little left of center is the Navy Yard's giant hammerhead crane.
Photo from the Emmerson Collection, courtesy Portsmouth Public Library

Under construction, the Downtown Tunnel—first under the Elizabeth River between Portsmouth and Norfolk—looks like a work of abstract art. Construction began in February 1950. The tube opened to traffic on May 23, 1952.
Mike Williams photo, courtesy Portsmouth Public Library

*The ferry entrance in Portsmouth in 1901 had separate gates for Norfolk-bound and Berkley-bound traffic.
Poster courtesy Everett Harrison*

The ferry City of Portsmouth *is shown on the Norfolk side of the Elizabeth River in 1901.
Photo courtesy Portsmouth Public Library*

*In 1940 a gold-lettered sign proudly proclaimed "Norfolk County Ferries, Est. 1636."
Photo courtesy Portsmouth Public Library*

A city worker in a cherry picker fastens a Christmas star, symbol of peace, atop a model of a rocket at the foot of High Street as Portsmouth decorates for the holiday season in 1960. The rocket was replaced with a new town clock, which, in turn, was replaced in the 1980s by a large, illuminated fountain.
Joseph T. McClenny photo, courtesy Portsmouth Public Library

A sign and a mourning wreath at the Portsmouth entrance signal the end of a 319-year-old institution as dusk deepens into night after the last ferry run on August 25, 1955.
Photo courtesy Portsmouth Public Library

To children the ferry captain seemed to ride majestically above everything else in the harbor. Many a child longed to be one.
Photo courtesy Portsmouth Public Library

The Isaac Fass Seafood dock and some of the fleet of fishing boats that served this prominent wholesaler are shown in 1933. Photo from the Emmerson Collection, courtesy Portsmouth Public Library

*The Circle Restaurant, 301 High Street, has been enlarged and remodeled several times since this 1958 view. Originally its curb service made it a great favorite with teenagers. Soon it became, and has remained, a great favorite among "family restaurants."
Photo courtesy Portsmouth Public Library*

*The morning sun strikes nineteenth-century facades on the west side of Court Street as viewed from Glasgow Street in this July 15, 1956 photo. A convenience store stands on the corner, next to the home of Miss Clyde White, veteran Woodrow Wilson High School teacher of English and journalism and advisor to The Student, a national award-winning school newspaper. Pigeons enjoy a bath in a Glasgow Street puddle.
Photo courtesy Portsmouth Public Library*

*The American National Bank stands on the northeast corner of High and Middle streets, its formal dignity not infringed by the Arthur Murray Dance Studios next door in 1958. The bank building was torn down in the 1970s but one of the lion's head arches was incorporated in the Memorial Arch erected by the Portsmouth Revolutionary Bicentennial Committee in Marquis de Lafayette Park on Crawford Street.
Photo from the Murdaugh Collection, courtesy Portsmouth Public Library*

*One of the most spectacular fires in Portsmouth history destroyed the old Seaboard warehouses on Febraury 21, 1958. Spectators crowd the scene as fire-fighting tugs futilely direct their hoses on the conflagration while the best efforts of firemen on land serve only to contain the blaze, not extinguish it. Despite the costliness of the fire, many would see it later as a blessing. In wiping out the old warehouses (below) it cleared the way for such waterfront brighteners as the Seawall Restaurant, Holiday Inn, and Harbor Tower.
Mike Williams photo,
courtesy Portsmouth Public Library*

*The southwest corner of Effingham and King streets, a predominantly black neighborhood, seems quiet for the Fourth of July, 1958. Maybe the neighborhood's residents are celebrating elsewhere.
Photo from the Murdaugh Collection, courtesy Portsmouth Public Library*

*The old bandstand on Afton Parkway in Cradock has become a symbol of that community. It has appeared on Portsmouth city stickers for automobiles. Cradock was part of ten square miles of Norfolk County territory annexed by the city in 1960.
Ramona H. Mapp photo*

*Though the Seawall and Portside are still in the future, the Holiday inn and its marina (foreground) and a high rise, Number One Crawford Parkway (far right), betoken a waterfront awakening in this photograph c. 1960. In the distance at left is the Navy Yard. Above the Holiday Inn, near the center of the picture, is a new Citizens Trust building under construction.
Ray Dolwick photo,
courtesy Portsmouth Public Library*

*The Misses Evelyn (left) and Lizzie (right) Hill flank Louise N. Fontaine (Mrs. Berkeley M.) in the Victorian back parlor of the Hills' home at 221 North Street. Miss Evelyn, last survivor of the family, conveyed Hill House to the Portsmouth Historical Association by deed of gift in November 1961. Maintained as the society's headquarters, the home is open to the public. The Hills also owned a beautiful Virginia Beach estate, Seabreeze Farms. A veteran teacher of history at Woodrow Wilson High School, Mrs. Fontaine was a major inspiration to generations of students, some of whom attained national and international distinction. Many of her former students still draw on her rich fund of anecdotes. To this day some Portsmouth residents are reminded of her—and of the glories of classical civilization—whenever they see a Doric, Ionic, or Corinthian column.
Photo courtesy Portsmouth Public Library*

*Of particular interest in the front parlor of Hill House are the pier glass and mirror over the fireplace.
Photo courtesy Portsmouth Public Library*

*This exterior picture reveals Hill House to be of the architectural style variously known as high basement, English basement, Hull, or Bristol-built. It is a Virginia Historic Landmark.
William J. Maloney photo*

*A bulldozer works amid shoreline rubble near the foot of High Street about 1962. More work is in progress farther along the shore. Work on the Seawall is still seven years in the offing. The old Seaboard Building, with its distinctive round facade, still serves as a municipal building and has not yet been redesigned for a restaurant, offices, and apartments. The model of a rocket in the cul de sac has not yet been replaced by the clock, which preceded the large fountain familiar today. The walkway from the circle to the Portsmouth Naval Shipyard museum is lined with historic cannon. Other guns are near the flagpole.
A Mike Williams photo,
courtesy Portsmouth Public Library*

*People launch their pleasure boats at Portsmouth City Park on a June day in 1961. The columned Federal portico of the home of Mr. and Mrs. George T. McLean is visible on the opposite shore in the Green Acres-Sterling Point section of Churchland. New boat ramps and other features of a park completely refurbished by 1988 now attract larger crowds to this facility.
Photo courtesy Portsmouth
Public Library*

*A delight to children in the 1960s and today, Pokey Smokey, a real little steam engine, carries them on a ride around part of City Park and into the world of romance. When small children hear the train's whistle in the distance, they insist that Pokey Smokey is calling them.
Dick Bruckse photo,
courtesy Portsmouth Public Library*

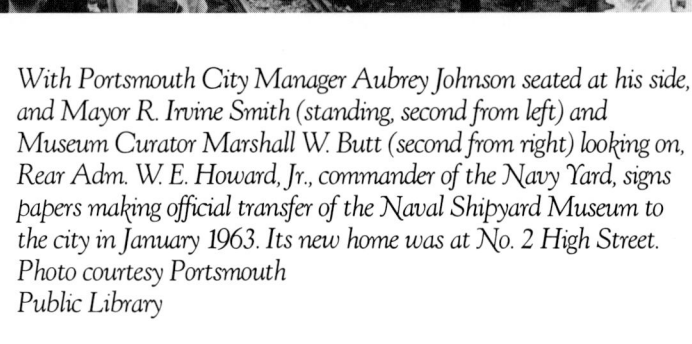

*With Portsmouth City Manager Aubrey Johnson seated at his side, and Mayor R. Irvine Smith (standing, second from left) and Museum Curator Marshall W. Butt (second from right) looking on, Rear Adm. W. E. Howard, Jr., commander of the Navy Yard, signs papers making official transfer of the Naval Shipyard Museum to the city in January 1963. Its new home was at No. 2 High Street.
Photo courtesy Portsmouth
Public Library*

*Vice Mayor Raymond Seward (center) cuts the ribbon with Herman (left) and Morris Rapoport at the opening of the Club Room in The Quality Shop in 1960. Herman's son Reid is the young boy in the background (between the vice mayor and Morris Rapoport). He is now co-owner of the prestigious men's furnishings store. Morris Rapoport founded the business in 1917 on small capital but great resourcefulness and dedication to quality. With too much money invested in straw hats that first summer, he had one frozen in a block of ice to promote cool headwear and sold out his stock. A prominent civic leader, recipient of an award from the National Conference of Christians and Jews, Morris Rapoport took a hand in the business almost until his death a few days short of what would have been his ninety-first birthday. His son, Herman, managed the firm successfully and in 1960 became the youngest president of the National Menswear Association. Under his leadership the firm opened a second store in 1963 in Norfolk's financial district. In the 1980s The Quality Shop was the first business to respond to City Manager Hanbury's appeal for restoration and renovation of High Street storefronts.
Photo courtesy The Qualty Shop*

*Representative Porter Hardy, Jr., and his wife read pleasing election news in their Churchland home. A Harvard-educated farmer and businessman, he was elected to Congress from the Second Congressional District in 1946. At that time the district included Portsmouth, Norfolk, South Norfolk, Suffolk, and the counties of Norfolk, Nansemond, Isle of Wight, and Princess Anne. The news here is not of his first election but a subsequent one. Though at the end of Mr. Hardy's first term the district had had five Congressmen in ten years (a national record for that period), he was re-elected repeatedly, serving until 1969. His twenty-two years in office were terminated at his wish, not his constituents'. Besides pleasing a district with often conflicting business, labor, and agricultural interests, he earned a national reputation as chairman of a House Armed Services Sub-committee investigating waste in federal operations.
Bob Morin photo,
courtesy Porter Hardy, Jr.*

The Portsmouth Coast Guard Lightship Museum, opened to the public in 1967, and the Holiday Inn appear in the left background of this 1960s scene. To the stern of the ship, Citizens Trust Bank rises from the horizon.
Herbert Barnes photo,
courtesy Portsmouth Public Library

A Portsmouth Chamber of Commerce delegation calls on Representative Porter Hardy, Jr., in his Capitol Hill office. Seated at the congressman's side is Joe Tusing, apparently chairman of the group. Mayor R. Irvine Smith stands behind the left rear corner of the desk. Standing third from left in front of the American flag is Superintendent of Schools M. E. Alford.
Photo courtesy Porter Hardy, Jr.

With William B. Spong, Jr., as a United States senator and Porter Hardy, Jr., as Second District representative, Portsmouth had a highly respected member in each chamber of the Congress. Spong was elected to a Senate term beginning in 1966.
Buddy Sanford photo,
courtesy Porter Hardy, Jr.

All of Portsmouth's problems—and those of the state, the nation, and the world—have been debated through the years by occupants of the Old Timers' Bench, outside the Court House Square at the northwest corner of High and Court streets. Members of the forum one day in 1955 were (from left to right) David Solomon, Jr.; John Davis; Eddie Cross; Herman Parker; Charles Lively; and Virgil Procter. At far right is the old Portsmouth Municipal Building, since demolished. Note the butt of an old cannon projecting from the sidewalk by the column at left.
Photo courtesy Portsmouth Public Library

Representative Hardy, Mayor R. Irvine Smith, State Senator Willard Moody, and United States Senator Spong confer on matters of concern to the city of Portsmouth at the opening of a new Social Security office on January 22, 1966.
Buddy Sanford photo,
courtesy Porter Hardy, Jr.

Willard J. Moody, of Portsmouth, served in the Virginia House of Delegates, 1956-1963, and in the State Senate, 1964-1984. He was chairman of the Senate Rules Committee and of the Senate Democratic Caucus.
Photo from O'Neal's Studio,
courtesy Willard J. Moody

storms

The great snowstorm of January 1918 gives downtown Portsmouth the look of a Midwestern town in winter. The view is up High Street, westward from the ferry. Photo from the Murdaugh Collection, courtesy Portsmouth Public Library

The temperate and generally non-violent climate of Hampton Roads has attracted many new businesses and residents and has been one factor in its generally high rating on various lists of best places to live. But Portsmouth has had snowstorms and a few great freezes, the more notable because of their rarity. A blizzard in January 1857 left some twenty-foot drifts. The Elizabeth River, frozen solid between Portsmouth and Norfolk, became the arena for ice skating and sleighing, and some enterprising soul opened a bar on the ice halfway between the two cities. Again, in the winter of 1917-1918, a solid field of ice stretched between Portsmouth and Norfolk. On that occasion, lanes were cut for the passage of ferries. And before completion of the Seawall in 1971 windstorms sometimes drove waters into some of the lower streets downtown.

As time passes, people tend to remember the adventurous part of weather emergencies more than the inconveniences. Here is a small album of weather pictures that may recall exciting moments.

A storm on August 23, 1933, floods large areas of the Navy Yard. Workers realized the shipyard had a close relationship with the sea but were not prepared for so encompassing an embrace.
Photo courtesy Portsmouth Public Library

The same storm transforms part of Court Street into a canal leading to the harbor. The two young men in the canoe (center, near the horizon) are Eddie Sam Maupin and the future Judge Winston Bain.
Photo courtesy Portsmouth Public Library

Water Street was given a surface true to its name by a storm of uncertain date that flooded the tracks of the Seaboard Air Line and provided a Venetian avenue to the old Portsmouth-Norfolk County Jail (right).
Photo courtesy Portsmouth Public Library

The Watts House (left, with historical marker) in early years had occupied a waterfront site. In the storm of August 6, 1957, the Elizabeth River came looking for its old companion.
Photo from the Murdaugh Collection, courtesy Portsmouth Public Library

An August 1953 storm left the barge Ontario *at the edge of Waverly Boulevard. Photo courtesy Portsmouth Public Library*

Before completion of the Seawall in 1971, a block of Dinwiddie Street sometimes became an inlet of the Elizabeth River. Photo courtesy Portsmouth Public Library

Except for the telephone poles and the automobiles, this January 12, 1962 view north up a snow-covered Crawford Street might have been photographed in the 1840s. Photo courtesy Portsmouth Public Library

A snowstorm in the 1950s blanketed Court Street and placed a white mantle on the shoulders of one Confederate soldier. Photo courtesy Portsmouth Public Library

Portside is a delight to Portsmouth residents, tourists, and Norfolk citizens who take the short ferry ride from their city's Waterside.
Dennis A. Mook photo

chapter fourteen
STIRRINGS OF PROGRESS

However progressive the city might be in some ways, for most of the 1960s the downtown area wore a depressing aspect. As new malls drew shoppers in increasing numbers, some store fronts grew shabby and others were boarded up. Rotting wharves and pilings gave a look of decay to the waterfront at the foot of High Street and for several blocks on either side.

In 1968 a new mayor, Jack P. Barnes, addressed the problem. His administration secured federal aid for construction of a seawall to hold back the waters that occasionally flooded some low-lying downtown streets. The city government had the foresight to provide a wall that was esthetically pleasing and that provided a breeze-swept walkway with fascinating views of the harbor. The structure not only became a popular promenade but also the site of the annual Seawall Art Show, which draws exhibitors and viewers from many states.

The Barnes administration also provided in 1970 a new, efficiently designed Civic Center to house the courts and city offices that had long since outgrown the 1846 Court House and other facilities. The new complex included a jail and police headquarters.

Mayor Barnes and the Council were mindful of blighted areas outside the downtown. One of these was Mt. Hermon, a predominantly black neighborhood that was rapidly becoming a slum. With the aid of federal funds and the cooperative efforts of the Council and many energetic residents, the Mt. Hermon Renewal Project became—and still remains—the largest achievement of its kind in Virginia.

In the years from 1968 to 1974, Barnes and the Council had begun to change the face of Portsmouth. They had initiated its recovery.

In those years a group of Portsmouth business and professional men had met frequently but informally to discuss the city's problems. They believed that Portsmouth's potential was perhaps as great as at any time in its history, but they were sure that there must be a broadening of the city's tax base if progress were to continue. In 1973 President Nixon and Secretary of State Kissinger had negotiated a ceasefire in Vietnam and it was widely predicted that a decline in Naval Shipyard employment would put a brake on Portsmouth's business growth. Everyone welcomed peace, but the circumstance emphasized the community's too heavy dependence on a single industry—moreover, on one completely dependent on fluctuations in foreign policy. A consistent leader in this group was Richard Davis, an energetic attorney and investment executive. In 1974 Davis, Edward L. Oast, Jr., and E. Saunders Early, Jr., ran for City Council on the same ticket.

The three pledged to seek means of diversifying the city's industry and broadening its tax base. They were elected and served with four other Council members, Jack Barnes, Robert W. Wentz, Jr., Dr. James W. Holley III, and Archie Elliott. The last two were black, Holley having shared with Raymond Turner in 1968 the distinction of being one of the first two members of his race elected to Portsmouth's governing body. Besides being bi-racial the new Council represented a variety of eocnomic and occupational interests; but despite sometimes sharp differences of opinion over issues before them, they were united in a vision of Portsmouth as a progressive city with a broadly

based economy. In those days the mayor was regularly elected by the Council from its own membership. This time Davis was chosen.

The Davis administration concentrated first on bringing a large oil refinery to the city but, because of delays resulting from the opposition of neighboring communities and a decline of such facilities as major agents of prosperity, the original dream was never realized. But a number of smaller industries and other businesses were attracted to Portsmouth. A change in the city charter provided for direct election of the mayor by the citizens beginning in 1976. Public approval of Davis was so strong that he was elected without opposition, serving until 1980. His greatest accomplishments were in stimulating a renewal of Portsmouth's spirit and making people elsewhere in Virginia and the nation aware that the city had shaken off its lethargy. He, and others working with him, convinced Portsmouth people that they could do great things. When Davis was elected lieutenant governor of Virginia in 1982, his success in Portsmouth had a lot to do with his victory.

Rotting pilings and wharf remains gave a look of decay to the downtown waterfront in the 1960s before building of the handsome Seawall pictured on page 203. The 1960s photo courtesy Portsmouth Public Library; the photo of the seawall is by Dennis A. Mook

In this 1968 close-up, the abandoned Portsmouth ferry slips and an adjacent wharf show considerable wear and tear. Photo courtesy Portsmouth Public Library

mayors of portsmouth

Portsmouth has not always had mayors. In 1763, the year after the death of its founder, Lt. Col. William Crawford, nine town trustees were named: Andrew Sprowle, George Veale, Charles Steuart, Humphrey Roberts, Francis Miller, James Roe, David Purcell, and Amos Etheridge.

In 1819 the town trustees were created a body corporate by an Act of the General Assembly of Virginia.

In 1852, when the town was a hundred years old, the town trustees were replaced by a mayor and council. Portsmouth was divided into two wards. All areas east of Court and Fourth streets composed Jackson and all of the remainder constituted Jefferson Ward.

Wards proliferated through the years until it was agreed in the 1940s that the ward system encouraged petty politics and denied a council seat to anyone who had the misfortune to live in a ward already held by a well-entrenched incumbent. Political scientists testified that city-wide elections would be more democratic than the ward system and would tend to result in selection of council members serving the city as a whole rather than a neighborhood constituency. The ward system was abolished.

The list of Portsmouth mayors is as follows:

1. John S. White, elected for one year, 1852; re-elected, 1853.
2. Hezekiah Stoakes, elected for one year, 1854.
3. D. D. Fiske, elected for one year, 1855.
4. George W. Grice, elected for one year, 1856.
5. James G. Hodges, elected for one year, 1857; re-elected 1858.
6. George W. Grice, again elected, 1859 and 1860.

R. Irvine Smith, mayor from 1960 to 1968, successfully pushed the program to give Portsmouth "the world's first completely planned container cargo port." He also was a stout friend of public education.
Herbert Barnes photo,
courtesy Portsmouth Public Library

7. John O. Lawrence, elected for one year, 1861.
8. John Nash, elected for one year, 1862; had served only one month when the city was placed under martial law.
9. Daniel Collins, elected under Federal military rule for one year, 1863; re-elected 1864 and 1865.
10. James C. White, elected for one year, 1866, under the Reconstruction Act. Mr. White served beyond the legal term for which he was elected.
11. James E. Stoakes, appointed under military occupation by Gen. John M. Schofield, May 1, 1868.
12. E. W. Whipple, appointed under military occupation by General Canby, October 5, 1869.
13. Philip G. Thomas, elected for one year, 1870; re-elected 1871.
14. A. S. Watts, elected for two years, 1872; re-elected 1874.
15. John O'Connor, elected for two years, 1876.
16. J. Thompson Baird, elected for two years, 1878; re-elected at each subsequent election until 1894.
17. L. H. Davis, elected for two years, 1894.
18. J. Thompson Baird, again elected for two years, 1896, and re-elected at each subsequent election until 1905.
19. J. Davis Reed, 1905-1912.
20. F. S. Hope, 1912-1916.
21. James T. Hanvey, 1916-1920.
22. R. A. Hutchins, Jr., 1920-1924.
23. L. G. White, 1924-1926.
24. Dr. Vernon A. Brooks, 1926-1932.
25. J. Alden Oast, 1932-1934.
26. Dr. Vernon A. Brooks, 1934-1936.
27. John P. Leigh, Sr., 1936-1944.
28. Leslie T. Fox, 1944-1950.
29. Fred A. Duke, 1950-1956.
30. A. C. Bartlett, 1956-1958.
31. B. W. Baker, 1958-1960.
32. R. Irvine Smith, 1960-1968.
33. Jack P. Barnes, 1968-1974.
34. Richard J. Davis, 1974-1980.
35. Julian E. Johansen, 1980-1984.
36. James W. Holley III, 1984-1987.
37. Gloria O. Webb, 1987-

Jack P. Barnes, Mayor from 1968 to 1974, who led the first successful efforts to halt decay of downtown Portsmouth. His administration secured federal aid for construction of the Seawall and obtained the Civic Center dedicated in 1970. He was president of the Virginia Municipal League for 1973-1974. As a councilman, he is still a strong advocate of economic development, education, and the arts. Photo courtesy Virginia Municipal League

Richard J. Davis, Mayor from 1974 to 1980, directed earnest efforts to enlarge the tax base, inspired Portsmouth people with the dream of a renewed city, and did a great deal to enhance Portsmouth's image in state and nation. Here Mayor Davis works in a Chicago hotel room, preparing his remarks on the occasion of Portsmouth being named an All-American City for 1975-1976. His success as mayor helped him to win election as lieutenant governor. As executive director of the Virginia Department of World Trade, he continues to work for the economic advancement of the area. Photo courtesy of Richard J. Davis

Rear Admiral Julian E. (Joe) Johansen, former commander of the Fifth Coast Guard District and a bank executive, was elected mayor in 1980 and served until 1984. He took the initiative in reestablishing ferry service between Portsmouth and Norfolk and pressed development of Portside on the downtown waterfront.
U.S. Coast Guard official photo

Gloria O. Webb, former chairwoman of the school Board and a Council member known for energetic support of education and the arts, became interim Mayor in 1987 and won a full term in 1988. She is the first woman to be mayor of the city.
Photo courtesy Gloria O. Webb

Dr. James W. Holley III, a dentist, long prominent civil rights leader, and one of Portsmouth's first two black members of City Council, served as mayor from 1984 to 1987. He was the first black mayor of the city.
Dennis A. Mook photo

During this same period, Portsmouth took pride in the political achievements of another native son, William B. Spong, Jr., United States Senator from 1966 to 1973. His scholarly and levelheaded progressivism quickly won respect in Washington.

Meanwhile, the senator's mother, the redoubtable Emily Spong, had been winning victories of her own. Petite, hatted, and white-gloved, she made her way from group to group, stirring concern for the preservation of the city's history and its architectural heritage. She was the driving spirit behind the Portsmouth Historical Foundation, a corporation chartered in 1963 to establish an historical zone in Olde Towne and offer inducements to individuals and corporations to buy and restore old buildings of historical or architectural value. In 1968, the City Council created a Board of Architectural Review to safeguard the eighteenth and nineteenth-century flavor of much of downtown Portsmouth. In 1970, through an effort sparked by Mrs. Spong, Olde Towne (Portsmouth Historic District), the 1846 Court House at High and Court streets, and the stone dry dock in the Naval Shipyard were all placed on the Virginia Landmarks Register and the National Register of Historic Places. A survey by the American Institute of Architects revealed that Portsmouth had a larger collection of architecturally noteworthy eighteenth and nineteenth-century houses than any other city on the East Coast of the United States between Alexandria and Georgetown on the north and Charleston, South Carolina, on the south.

For 1975-1976 Portsmouth received the coveted All-America City designation of the National League of Municipalities. The official citation said that the community merited the distinction not because it had fewer problems than other cities, but because it had worked to solve them with uncommon goodwill and resourcefulness. High in its praise of the municipal government, the jury said that equal credit should go to various civic organizations.

In 1976 John Warner, then executive director of the American Revolution Bicentennial Administration, traveled to Portsmouth to present the National Bicentennial Medal to the city's American Revolutionary Bicentennial Committee. Before a luncheon gathering of several hundred city officials and civic leaders, Warner said that the award recognized the committee's "creation and execution of programs unexcelled by any city in the United States."

The committee had been created in 1968 and functioned into 1981. Highlights of the observance included a Hampton Roads Anglo-American Friendship Day featuring British Ambassador Sir Peter Ramsbotham, erection and dedication of a Lafayette Arch, dedication of a monument commemorating Cornwallis's embarkation from Portsmouth for Yorktown, many educational and musical programs, publications, and radio and television presentations. Some of the Portsmouth celebrations received media coverage in every state in the Union.

In June 1984 the 1846 Court House, on the northwest corner of High and Court streets, was dedicated to use as a museum. Tenantless for several years after being vacated by the courts, the building had faced demolition. Two Portsmouth women, Mrs. Emily Spong and Mrs. Robert Brooke Albertson, aroused their fellow citizens and circulated petitions to preserve the structure. The Portsmouth Museum and Fine Arts Commission secured use of the building and, under the guidance of John Paul Hanbury, a prominent architect, its exterior was restored to its 1890s appearance while the interior was converted to use as a children's museum on the first floor and an art gallery on the second.

At dedication ceremonies the chairman of the Museum and Fine Arts Commission predicted that the restored Court House would become "the linchpin of Portsmouth's cultural life." So it proved. It was soon the scene of the city's first world premiere—that of the traveling exhibit of the *Mary Rose*. The Portsmouth event attracted 45,793 viewers, was publicized internationally, and drew a letter of commendation from the Prince of Wales. A presentation of Chinese art, opened by the Chinese ambassador, gave Portsmouth people the first look at an important national exhibit. Other displays, some of national or international interest, some attuned especially to regional or local concerns, gave proof of a revitalized art scene. Historical displays dealing with everything from the Navy and Coast Guard to the railroads, bygone scenes in Portsmouth, and archaeological finds from Tudor England gave variety to the museum scene. The city's five museums—the Court House Gallery, the Children's Museum, the Community Arts Center, the Naval Museum, and the Coast Guard Lightship Museum—attracted unprecedented crowds. For two successive years, 1984 and 1985, the Portsmouth museums received the Downtown Merchants Award for the person or agency contributing most to the downtown area.

The whole process of refurbishing downtown Portsmouth, which had declined in the face of growing malls, was greatly augmented by the vision and enthusiasm of George L. Hanbury II, who became city manager on July 15, 1982. Hanbury was a strong supporter of cultural growth, both because of its economic significance as an attracter of industry and tourists and its life-enhancing value to Portsmouth's own citizens. He also emphasized beautification, especially of the downtown area and of the avenues by which people entered the city. In both of these programs, he had the support of City Council. Today Portsmouth offers more cultural opportunities to all its people than ever before in its history and the downtown area is more attractive than at any other time in the memory of most citizens.

City officials and Chamber of Commerce leaders decided that Portsmouth would do well to be an Alexandria to Norfolk's Washington. The smaller city could benefit in many ways from being part of the metropolitan area but it could find satisfaction, and attract desirable citizens, by retaining its own flavor. Though it had a few highrises and various structures typical of modern development elsewhere in the United States and abroad, old Portsmouth retained many distinctive features. A person parachuted into it blindfolded would not think, upon having the blindfold removed, that he could be in any of a thousand other communities.

The charm of Olde Towne and of the restored and refurbished downtown business area reflects the eighteenth, nineteenth, and twentieth-century experiences of the city. A growing number and variety of restaurants attract residents of neighboring cities who like to dine on Tidewater seafood, traditional Southern cooking, continental cuisine, or oriental fare amid surroundings ranging from the classic cafe through colonial and Victorian to the glamor of glittering art deco. Night-time entertainment ranges from classic films to variety acts in restored theaters and modern restaurants. Portsmouth's festive Portside is designed to complement the attractions of Norfolk's Waterside. The 1840s-style ferries are kept busy shuttling between the two attractions.

Some people employed in Norfolk's financial district have moved to Portsmouth, enjoying the ambience of the smaller city and finding a ferry ride to work preferable to the chore of driving. In 1987, no less than 784,555 people rode the ferries.

Portsmouth's resurgence is by no means confined to the downtown. Churchland, an area of choice residential property at the opposite end of High Street, is hailed by economic analysts and realtors as the fastest growing section of the city and one of the three most promising areas in all of Hampton Roads.

Portsmouth Pride—an effort initiated by the Chamber of Commerce to foster and publicize the city's attractions—has been a huge success. The ease with which the program surpassed by $200,000 its original 1983 goal of raising $1 million, and then proceeded to campaign in 1987 for another million, is conspicuous proof of the vitality of Portsmouth's citizens and of their faith in the city's destiny.

Statistical evidence of the city's recent progress is available. Although the 1970 federal census showed a drop in population since 1960 and the 1980 census showed a further drop from 110,963 in 1970 to 104,577, the Census Bureau's interim estimate in 1986 showed a rise to 111,000.

As Portsmouth moves toward the 1990s it enjoys many advantages from being part of Hampton Roads. It is part of a metropolitan area with one of the highest employment rates in the United States and with a per capita income consistently above the national average. Besides enriching Hampton Roads with its own attractions, Portsmouth enjoys a more pleasant lifestyle because of the attractions of neighboring cities, particularly the outstanding museums in Norfolk, Virginia Beach, Hampton, and Newport News; the recreation facilities and musical organizations of Virginia Beach; and such Norfolk-based institutions as the Virginia Stage Company, Virginia Opera, and the Virginia Symphony. Such great national tourist attractions as Williamsburg, Jamestown, and Yorktown are only a short drive away.

■

Year	Land Area (Sq. Mi.)	Population
1752	0.2	Unknown
1763	0.5	Unknown
1784	.07	Unknown
1790	0.7	1,700
1840	0.7	6,577
1850	0.7	8,626
1860	0.7	9,496
1870	0.7	10,590
1880	0.7	11,390
1890	0.7	13,268
1900	1.4	17,427
1910	2.4	33,190
1920	5.8	54,387
1930	5.8	45,704
1940	5.8	50,745
1950	9.7	80,039
1960	18.8	114,775
1970	30.0	110,963
1980	30.0	104,577
1986	30.0	111,000

Source: U.S. Census Bureau

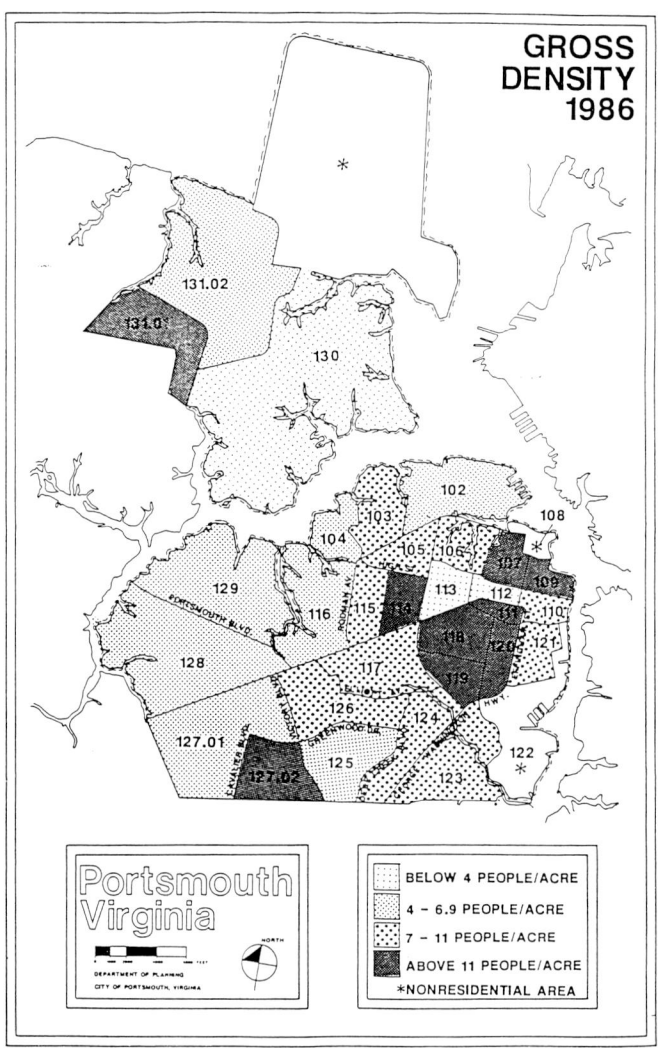

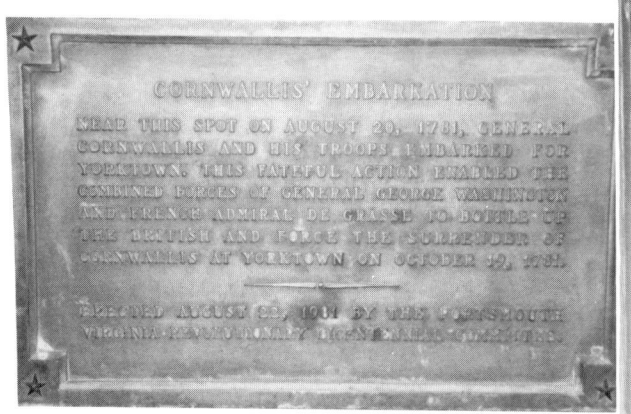

Plaques of the Lafayette Arch (right) and the memorial commemorating British General Lord Cornwallis's embarkation (above) from Portsmouth for Yorktown. Both monuments were erected by the Portsmouth Revolutionary Bicentennial Committee, which in 1976 received the National Bicentennial Medal for "planning and execution of programs of a quality unexcelled in any city in the United States."
Ramona H. Mapp photos

City Manager G. Robert House, two members of his administration, and the policeman piloting the plane were killed when their craft crashed on May 28, 1982. Mr. House had been in office only about a year, but he enjoyed a high national reputation in his profession and his performance in Portsmouth had raised great hopes.
Photo courtesy Mrs. G. Robert House

The handsome Seawall replaced wharf wreckage which moved the downtown shoreline in the 1960s.
Dennis A. Mook photo

Portsmouth dedicates its new Civic Center in 1970. At the microphone is Mayor Jack P. Barnes. On the front row of the speakers' stand are, from left to right, Leslie L. Fry (bearded), architect Glenn Yeats, William B. Spong, Jr., and Virginia Attorney General Andrew Miller. In the second row, between Spong and the Attorney General, is Margarette Miller, director of the Bellamy Foundation.
Harold P. Grant photo, courtesy Jack P. Barnes

The Carrie B. waits at the dock in downtown Portsmouth as a smaller harbor tour boat chugs past. The Navy Yard's hammer crane is prominent in the background.
Photo courtesy Portsmouth Public Library

Coleman's Nursery is not only a major dealer in plants but famed for acres of animated Christmas displays drawing visitors from many communities in Virginia and North Carolina. On New Year's Eve 1982 its principal building and a major part of the displays, patiently constructed over the years by Coleman's employees, were destroyed by fire. The nursery had provided a meeting room for local organizations and had been public-spirited in many ways. Organizations and individuals raised money to help the owners repair a loss only partially covered by insurance. In spring of 1983 the General Assembly of Virginia presented Coleman's a resolution recognizing its long service to the community. On October 1, 1983, Coleman's reopened in a new building on the old site and in the holiday season new animated displays, and a few old survivors, greeted delighted children and their parents.
Photos courtesy Coleman's Nursery

Popularity of the Carrie B. harbor cruise suggested to Mayor Johansen and other city officials that the public might be ready for revival of ferry service between Portsmouth and Norfolk. The sister city joined Portsmouth's initiative and the Elizabeth River ferry was reborn. The new vessel somewhat resembled the old Gosport, which was placed in service on March 9, 1832, and excited admiration by running "from wharf to wharf in five minutes." According to a contemporary account: "A sad accident marked the initial trip, one of the Portsmouth passengers mistaking the cylinder exhaust valves for a speaking tube. He was shortly afterwards presented with a set of false teeth by the sympathetic officials of the ferry." One can only hope that the writer, like some of today's newspaper columnists, was indulging in hyperbole for humorous effect.
William J. Maloney photo

A reproduction of the Cradock Bandstand was Portsmouth's symbol at the National League of Municipalities convention at which the city received the coveted All-American award.
Photo courtesy Portsmouth Public Library

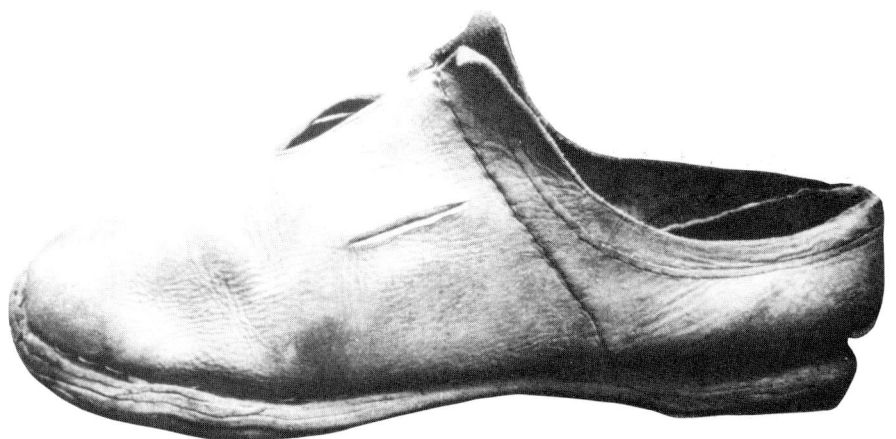

This shoe is from the foot of an English sailor who lost his life when the Mary Rose, "the jewel in the crown of Henry VIII's Navy," suddenly keeled over and sank on "a sparkling summer's morning in 1545." This shoe and the pewter objects shown here are among the artifacts from the ship which were seen by 45,793 people at Portsmouth's world premier of the Mary Rose Traveling Exhibit. The event attracted international attention and prompted a letter of commendation from His Royal Highness, the Prince of Wales. Dennis A. Mook photos

Gov. Charles Robb chats with Alf J. Mapp, Jr., chairman of the Museums and Fine Arts Commission, and Mayor Holley at the first night of Portsmouth's world premiere of the Mary Rose exhibit in June 1985.
Dennis A. Mook photo

Dedication of the 1846 Court House in June 1984 as an art gallery and children's museum was a major force in revitalizing the downtown. For two successive years the Portsmouth Museums received the Downtown Merchants Association Award to the individual or organization most responsible for improvements in the area. A new director of museums, Dr. Nancy Melton, took office on July 1, 1984, and inaugurated a series of exhibits that drew state, national, and international attention to Portsmouth.
Frankee Spurling photo

*Sir David Hannay, British Minister to the United States, talks with City Manager George L. Hanbury II in June 1985 at ceremonies for the unveiling of the statue of Henry VIII as an addition to the Mary Rose exhibit. While Sir David was in Portsmouth, announcement came of his appointment as British ambassador to the European Community. Later he was president of its Council.
Dennis A. Mook photo*

*The annual Seawall Art Show draws Portsmouth residents and out-of-town visitors. Rising tall in the left background is Harbor Tower with apartments affording spectacular views of the harbor. Passing boats vie for attention with the art on display. The lantern-topped mast of the Coast Guard Lightship Museum is between Harbor Tower and an old-fashioned lamp post. In the right background is the Norfolk skyline.
Dennis A. Mook photo*

*AFL-CIO headquarters in Portsmouth are in a fine old building on the southwest corner of Court Street and London Boulevard. One of the city's prime economic assets is a reservoir of skilled labor.
Ramona H. Mapp photo*

*Yachts and cabin cruisers fill the Holiday Inn Marina and dot the harbor off downtown Portsmouth.
Dennis A. Mook photo*

Men in Revolutionary garb fire a Fourth of July salute in front of the 1846 Court House.
Dennis A. Mook photo

Portsmouth's mounted police, a familiar and helpful presence in the downtown, are part of a High Street parade.
Dennis A. Mook photo

Governor Gerald Baliles; Han Xu, Peoples Republic of China ambassador to the United States; Museum Director Nancy Melton; and Ge Qiyun, Chinese Embassy official and wife of the ambassador, view an internationally publicized exhibit of Chinese art at the 1846 Court House on opening night March 9, 1986. Before the ceremonies, Ambassador Han and Governor Baliles dined in a Portsmouth home, Willow Oaks, and inaugurated trade negotiations between Virginia and China.
J. R. Murray photo

The fountain at the foot of High Street is a pleasantly cool sight on a summer day.
Dennis A. Mook photo

some neighborhoods and homes

Some Portsmouth neighborhoods exemplify modernity, some tradition, and some a blending of the two. Together they compose the mosaic that is Portsmouth.

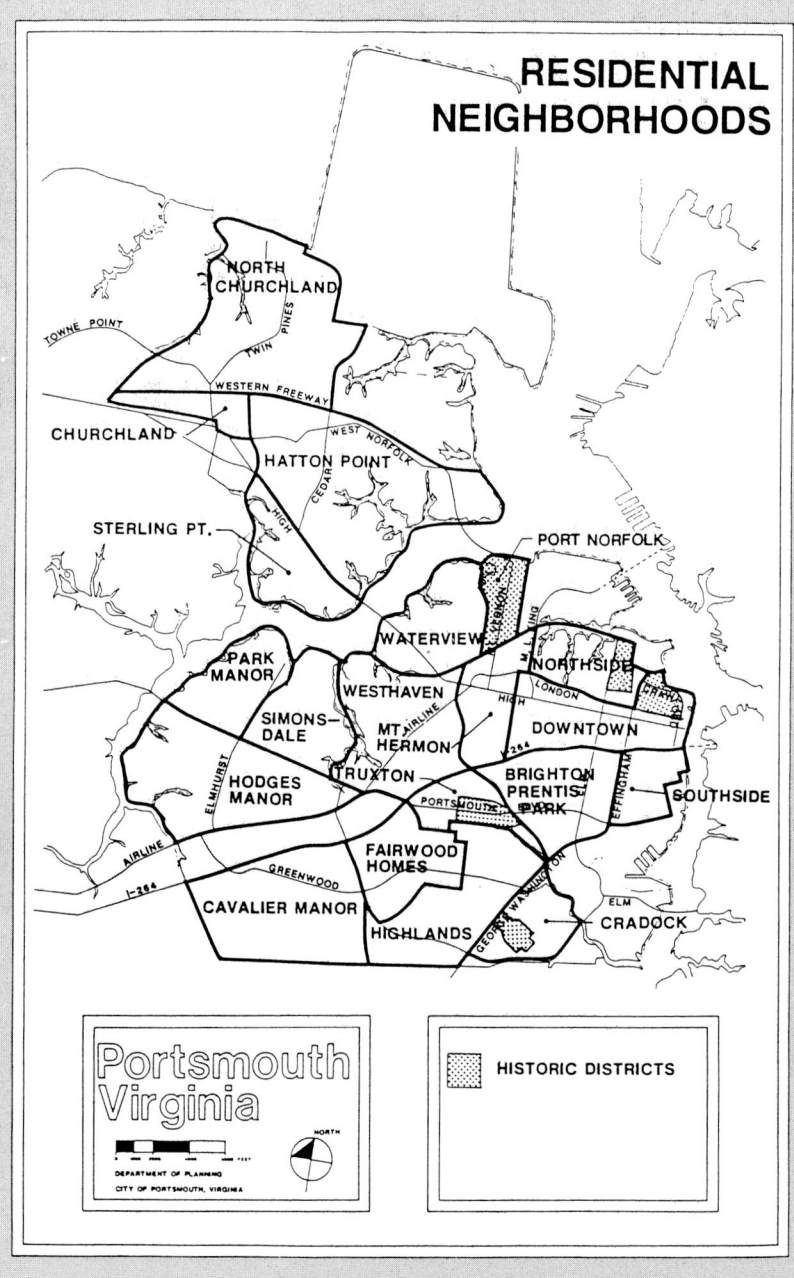

OLDE TOWNE
Tradition predominates architecturally in Olde Town.

1.

2.

*The two cast-iron dogs have been very much at home in several Portsmouth neighborhoods. Countless children have climbed upon their backs in a ritual wearing off many coats of paint. Here they guard the front steps of a house on Dinwiddie Street (1), where their tour of duty lasted through the 1930s and beyond. In 1898 they flanked the "ladies" entrance to the Ocean House Hotel (2). Today, their chests painted white, they greet visitors to a home on Grayson Street in Waterview. Siblings of these iron dogs are sentries at the main entrance to the Bartlett Hayward Plant of Koppers Company, Inc., of Baltimore, where they are believed to bring good luck. The company's researchers say that the dogs were cast by their firm in the 1850s and represented Sailor and Canton, live Newfoundland dogs brought to the Chesapeake Bay country by George Law in 1807. Sailor, it is said, went to Gov. Edward Lloyd on Maryland's Eastern Shore and Canton to Dr. James Stewart of Sparrows Point on the Western Shore. Generations of independent breeding from the two sires, with hounds and spaniels, produced dogs so much alike that the two strains were recognized in 1877 as constituting a separate breed, the Chesapeake Bay Retriever.
Photos courtesy Portsmouth Public Library; the dogs photo is from the Emmerson Collection*

Two London Street houses evoke the spirit of old Portsmouth. The one on the right is a perfect example of the English basement, or Bristol-built, house. To the left is the Cassell house, built about 182. by Captain John W. McRae, believed to have been lost at sea during the construction. The house passed to the Cassell family, long prominent in Portsmouth affairs, and is still identified with that family by many Portsmouth natives.
William J. Maloney photo

The Washington Reed house, on the southeast corner of Middle and North streets, looks today as it does in this early 1950s photo, although one is not likely now to find a horse-drawn cart at the curb.
Photo courtesy Portsmouth Public Library

The house on the northwest corner of North and Middle streets was built about 1792 by Dr. William Leigh and purchased in 1810 by Swepson Whitehead, one of the founding trustees of Portsmouth Academy. The home was made into a double house after the Civil War, but was reconverted to a single family residence in the 1900s and was for many years the home of the late Dr. and Mrs. Russell M. Cox.
Photo from the Murdaugh Collection, courtesy Portsmouth Public Library

A restored Irish row house, one remaining of four, stands on the southwest corner of Crawford and Glasgow streets.
Photo courtesy Portsmouth Public Library

The west side of Court Street, as seen by one looking north from the intersection with Glasgow in 1953, is little different from the view thirty-five years earlier or thirty-five years later.
Photo from the Murdaugh Collection, courtesy Portsmouth Public Library

The upper part of the restored home at 215 Glasgow Street was the old market house that stood in the middle of the first block of High Street before 1835.
William J. Maloney photo

Few Old Towne houses are more boldly individualistic than the fortress-like Victorian Romanesque structure (below) on the southeast corner of Court and North streets. Originally an Armistead house, it was long the home of the Elks before conversion into apartments in the 1970s.
Ramona H. Mapp photo

PARK VIEW

Two interesting residences face each other across Hatton Street. The Ionic-columned portico of one suggests an antebellum plantation house, though apparently conversion to apartments has resulted in uncharacteristic fenestration in the classical pediment (above, right). The other is a classic example of American Gothic.
Alf J. Mapp, Jr. photos

211

CAVALIER MANOR

Two modern homes nestle among the pines in Cavalier Manor.
Ramona H. Mapp photo

PORT NORFOLK

A Victorian-turreted house (above) on Bayview Boulevard in the Port Norfolk section of Portsmouth looks across the waters to West Norfolk. Several such homes remain on the boulevard and are much cherished now that the neighborhood is a historic district and restoration has been given a high priority.
Ramona H. Mapp photo

GLENSHEALLAH

Facing each other across Park Road in Glensheallah are two homes representative of the neighborhood's prevalently traditional architecture.
Ramona H. Mapp photo

PARK MANOR

The front windows of this house on Pennington Drive look out upon a well-kept yard. A balcony on the rear overlooks the Western Branch of the Elizabeth River.
Ramona H. Mapp photo

CHURCHLAND

The boyhood home of Capt. Stephen Carney (1810-1890) is in Sweetbriar at the end of Ferguson Drive. Captain Carney often adjudicated, from his front porch, chancery disputes that his neighbors would otherwise have carried to court. It is said that his rulings were never rejected.
Ramona H. Mapp photo

The backyard of this house (below) on Sterling Point Drive slopes to an arm of the Western Branch of the Elizabeth River.

These two homes are on adjacent lots on Tanbark Lane, which is almost like a rural enclave in the midst of the city. The white-columned, Virginia Colonial home is built on a point of land projecting into the Western Branch of the Elizabeth River but also adjacent to a lake. The Tidewater Georgian home, Willow Oaks, faces the lake and has a backyard sloping to the river, so that water is visible from each of its forty windows.
Ramona H. Mapp photos

ELIZABETH MANOR

Reflections in a lake double the beauty of this Elizabeth Manor house and its grounds.
Ramona H. Mapp photo

Lawns in Elizabeth Manor, like these at the water's edge, are almost as well manicured as those at the nearby golf course.
Alf J. Mapp, Jr. photo

High Street, looking west from the waterfront, 1988.
J. R. Murray photo

chapter fifteen
THE FUTURE

Scheduled for completion by the end of 1991 are three major transportation links that will place Portsmouth in the center of communication for Southeastern Virginia. One of these—a third crossing of Hampton Roads, in addition to the bridge-tunnel between Hampton and Norfolk and the James River Bridge between Suffolk and Newport News—will bring Portsmouth within minutes of both Newport News and Hampton. It is estimated that, by the year 2000, this route will be used daily by sixty thousand vehicles.

These developments in Hampton Roads come at a time when the Commonwealth of Virginia is taking enormous strides culturally and economically. Its state university system, by almost any test, is one of the tiny handful of most respected in the nation. In population the commonwealth, with 5.9 million residents, has forged ahead of Massachusetts and Indiana to rank twelfth among the fifty states. In per capita income it stands eleventh. As Gov. Gerald Baliles pointed out in a State of the Commonwealth message in 1988, if Virginia were a separate nation its gross national product would surpass that of Denmark, Austria, and the Union of South Africa to place it eighteenth among the countries of the world.

If Portsmouth's city government, business community, labor unions, and individual citizens can work together in the spirit of cooperation that was the primary factor in winning the All-American City designation, the future of the community will probably be brighter than any of the past eras whose accomplishments we now honor. Portsmouth, Virginia, is an exciting place to be as the 1980s slide into the 1990s and the world moves toward the dawn of a new century.

■

The former Pythian Castle, a Court Street building of exotic architecture, has been restored and now houses a French bakery and delicatessen.
Wiliam J. Maloney photo

The Commodore Theater, when it opened in the 400 block of High Street in 1945, was the best equipped and most comfortable movie emporium in Hampton Roads. Its name honors Commodore James Barron whose tomb is in the adjacent Trinity Episcopal Church burial ground, a portion of whose ancient wall is visible at left. The theater was still flourishing when this picture was taken in 1961 but fell upon bad days and eventually was closed. In 1988 it is being refurbished and its murals of Hampton Roads scenes are being restored so that it may be operated as a cabaret-style movie theater. Photo from the Murdaugh Collection, courtesy Portsmouth Public Library

Beyond the Seawall, Portsmouth's Harbor Tower rises like a monolith. J. R. Murray photo

Across green fields in the West Norfolk area of Portsmouth lies the new Cogentrix steam-generating plant which will furnish steam power to Virginia Chemicals, a major Portsmouth industry with international affiliations, and generate electricity for Virginia Power. The plant is on the Beazley estate, a former Carney plantation.
Dennis A. Mook photo

Port Centre (middle ground of this aerial photo), a 70-acre Commerce Park between downtown and the Navy Yard in 1988, occupies the former location of the city's worst slums. City analysts estimate that the development should create 1,900 jobs and generate $1.2 million a year in municipal taxes.
Dennis A. Mook photo

portsmouth's national notables

An editorial suggestion from the *Virginian-Pilot* that Portsmouth had produced more than its share of national and international figures prompted the Portsmouth Partnership to sponsor "A Notable Occasion," a celebration October 11-17, 1987, honoring outstanding achievers born or reared in the city. The municipal government and WAVY-TV joined in honoring the "exemplars of excellence."

Twenty-eight honorees were selected after a careful survey by the Portsmouth Notables Committee: Chairman Junius H. Williams, Jr., B. Jane Garrett, Abe Goldblatt, Alice C. Hanes, Raymond A. Peabody, Sheila P. Pittmann, Glenn Allen Scott, John T. Stone, and Faith W. Stuart. Of the twenty-five living honorees, seven—Allen, Davis, Glover, Harper, l'Anson, Mapp, and Parker—were still in Portsmouth.

The photos that follow, with the exception of those of Spong and Mapp, are the same that appeared in printed programs for the occasion. All biographical sketches were excerpted from the same source where, as here, they appeared in alphabetical order.

1. Dr. Mac Carter Adams

2. Rear Adm. Edward C. Allen, Jr.

3. Virginia C. Andrews

4. Marty Brennaman

5. Ruth Weston Brown

6. Robert H. Buckner

7. Mahlon Clark

8. Ralph Wolfe Cowan

217

9. Richard J. Davis

10. Dr. Julian M. Earls

11. Perry Ellis

12. David Carr Glover

13. Chandler Harper

14. Charles F. Harris

15. W. Nathaniel Howell

16. Lawrence W. I'Anson

17. G. Douglas Johnston

18. Junius Kellogg

19. Rear Adm. Herman Joseph Kossler

20. Frank D. Lawrence

21. Alf Johnson Mapp, Jr.

22. Tommy Newsom

23. Dr. James Cuthbert Owens

24. Clarence "Ace" Parker

25. William Schneider
26. William B. Spong, Jr.
27. Theodore Taylor
28. Lt. Gen. Wm. G. Townsend Tuttle, Jr.

1
Dr. Mac Carter Adams. *Former Deputy Under Secretary of Defense for tactical warfare programs.* As an aeronautical engineer, Adams was associate administrator of the Office of Advanced Research and Technology at NASA headquarters in Washington. He was responsible for the management of research and technology programs encompassing a budget of $500 million.

While at AVCO, Adams designed a heat shield that eliminated the technical problems of re-entry into Earth's atmosphere. In 1961, he was elected one of the ten Outstanding Young Men in America for his work with intercontinental ballistic missiles.

As deputy undersecretary of defense, Adams was the link between the congressional Appropriations and Armed Services Committees and the armed forces acquisitions of tactical-weapon systems.

2
Rear Adm. Edward C. Allen, Jr. *Commander of the Fifth Coast Guard District, 1967-71.*

During World War II, Allen was serving on the Alexander Hamilton when it was torpedoed and sank off the coast of Iceland in 1942. He was later aboard the attack troop transport Leonard Wood in the invasions of North Africa, Sicily, and nine Pacific islands. He commanded three Coast Guard vessels and held two major Coast Guard commands in Europe. He received the Bronze Star, nine battle stars and a Navy Citation for his services.

3
Virginia C. Andrews. *Author.* Best known for her series of stories about the fate of the Dollanganger children hidden for years in their hateful grandmother's attic. The novels have been sold worldwide and translated into as many as sixteen languages.

Andrews was the number one bestseller paperback original author for 1984 and 1985. All novels have been multimillion copy bestsellers and all have been on the New York Times *bestseller list for more than 3 ½ months.* Andrews is deceased.

4
Marty Brennaman. *Broadcaster.* The sports announcer who broadcasts all of the Cincinnati Reds' Games, Brennaman began his broadcasting career in television in High Point, North Carolina. He later returned to WTKR radio in Norfolk to broadcast the Squires basketball games. During his years at WTKR he was selected Virginia's Sportcaster of the Year on four occasions. In 1974, he joined the Red's broadcasting team.

5
Ruth Weston Brown. *A top rhythm-and-blues vocalist of the 1950s.* Known as Miss Rhythm, she recorded on the Atlantic and Phillips labels. She has several gold hits and received a Grammy nomination in 1969 for her rendition of the Beatles' hit "Yesterday."

After many successful years Ms. Brown settled down to rear her family. She began to rebuild her career after her sons entered college. She began playing in clubs again and toured Japan with the Thad Jones-Mel Lewis Orchestra.

Ms. Brown soon discovered a new career—acting. She enrolled in a drama workshop and landed a part in a play, Living Fat, portraying an eighty-two-year-old woman. Ms. Brown was spotted by Norman Lear who urged her to do a screen test for the series "Hello Lany." She got the part and was signed on as a semi-regular. She was also featured in the Chevy Chase film Under the Rainbow.

6
Robert H. Buckner. *Screen writer and producer for fifty-seven pictures in thirty-six years.* Among his best films are Knute Rockne—All American, a 1940 film starring Ronald Reagan and Yankee Doodle Dandy, the story of George M. Cohan that won an Academy Award for James Cagney in 1942.

Buckner is possibly the only former foreign correspondent alive who interviewed Adolf Hitler, Stalin, Mussolini, Haile Selassie, and the ex-Kaiser Wilhelm II of Germany for the London Daily Mail and the New York World newspapers.

Buckner has recently finished a screenplay for International Film Productions in Paris. He has also launched a new and successful career, painting "Semi-representational" oils and acrylics.

7
Mahlon Clark. *A clarinetist who is best remembered locally as a member of the Lawrence Welk band.*

Clark was fifteen years old when he began playing with bands professionally around the Portsmouth and Norfolk areas. After graduating from Wilson, he went on the road and spent a year touring the South with Dean Hudson's Territory Band. In 1941, at the age of eighteen, Clark joined the Will Bradley Band. He later played with Ray McKinley, Phil Harris, Bob Crosby, Tex Beneke's Glenn Miller Band, and Lawrence Welk. For fifteen years he has been recorded with various jazz groups, big bands, movies, and television shows. He just finished an album iwth his own jazz combo. He works on jazz concerts nationwide, and during the past twenty-five years he has worked in hundreds of TV shows, and movies, recording background music.

8
Ralph Wolfe Cowan. *Portrait painter.* Cowan received his first big break in 1956 when Prince Ranier III awarded him the title of Royal Portrait Painter to Monaco as a result of his life-size portrait of the newly crowned Princess Grace. He returned to Monaco some twenty-five years later to paint the entire royal family.

Cowan is now working on his first-ever series of "non-portraits" for collectors and the fine print market.

9
Richard J. Davis. *Business leader and public official.*

Chairman of the board and president of Virginia Investment and Mortgage Corporation, which started in 1954. He is currently a member of the legislative committee for the Mortgage Bankers Association of America and former vice-president of that Association. While serving as the Mayor of Portsmouth from 1974-1980, he was chairman of the Housing and Community Development Committee for the United States Conference of Mayors. In 1981, Davis became the lieutenant governor of Virginia. He also served as chairman of the Democratic Party of Virginia.

Davis has been chairman of many successful fundraising campaigns, including the campaign to raise funds for the Martha W. Davis Cancer Center in Portsmouth.

10
Dr. Julian M. Earls. *Chief of the Health, Safety and Security Division of NASA Lewis Research Center, Cleveland, Ohio.* Dr. Earles is responsible for a staff of over one hundred people in the areas of occupational medicine, environmental health, industrial safety, radiation physics, classified security, and computer security.

Dr. Earls was included in the first group voted into the National Black College Hall of Fame along with Dr. Martin Luther King, Jr.; Leontyne Price; and Justice Thurgood Marshall.

He is the founder of an organization whose numbers pledge one thousand dollars a year for life to raise scholarship funds for black students who attend black colleges.

11
Perry Ellis. *Fashion designer.* Ellis quickly became known internationally. He was the recipient of eight Coty Awards and was twice voted into the Coty Hall of Fame. He also received the American Sportswear Award of the Council of Fashion Designers and the Neiman-Marcus Award for distinguished service to the fashion industry. Ellis is deceased.

12
David Carr Glover, Jr. A music teacher, composer, and arranger, best known for his arrangement of the "Mickey Mouse March" and other Disney classics. He founded the Tidewater Music Teachers Forum, a local music teachers' organization with both state and national affiliations.

In 1967, the David Carr Glover Piano Library was published after being pre-tested for many years with local piano students. It is a piano teaching course (also available for organ) designed for beginners and advanced players and published in eight languages. His published catalogue at the present includes over one thousand books and hundreds of original solos with sales of over a million copies annually.

Glover has also arranged piano editions of music from movies, Broadway shows, and television productions such as The Sound of Music, A Chorus Line, Camelot, The Sting, "Magnum PI," "The Hulk," E. T., Annie, and Fiddler on the Roof.

He is presently under contract with Columbia Pictures Publications, a division of Coca-Cola.

13
J. Chandler Harper *won the 1950 Professional Golfers Association Tournament and was inducted into the PGA Hall of Fame in 1969.*

In 1930, at age sixteen, Harper first won the Virginia State Amateur Championship, a title he won three times. In 1932, at age eighteen, he became the youngest winner of the State Open. He was also the oldest winner in 1970, at age fifty-six. He won the title a record ten times. He has won numerous other tournaments, including the Texas Open, the El Paso Open, the Tucson Open, and the Mid-Atlantic Professional Golf Association Championship. He is also a former member of the United States Ryder Cup Team.

In 1965, at age fifty-one, Harper won the United States Seniors' title in Las Vegas. In 1968, he won the World Senior title at Downfield Golf Club in Scotland, where he still serves as honorary president.

14
Charles F. Harris. *Founder of Amistad Press, Inc., a publishing company.*

Mr. Harris began his career in 1956 at Doubleday & Co., Inc., and later became supervisor of analysis and research.

In 1965, he originated the Zenith Book series, textbooks used in secondary social studies and English courses in the United States to present a history of America's minorities.

He was senior editor of the Adult Trade Division of Random House from 1967 to 1971. While holding this position, he originated the concept of Amistad, a paperback publication for use in college-level social science and humanities courses. Each volume has sold over thirty-five thousand copies.

In 1980, Mr. Harris established the Howard University Press Book Publishing Institute, a five-week workshop for students interested in careers in publishing. It is the only publishing workshop operated by a university press.

15
W. Nathaniel Howell. *Ambassador to Kuwait.*

Before joining the Foreign Service in 1965, Howell was an instructor in government and foreign affairs at the University of Virginia for one year. His first assignment as a junior officer was executive assistant to the ambassador in Cairo. From 1967 to 1968 he served as political officer to the United States Mission to the North Atlantic Treaty Organization in Paris and Brussels. He returned to Washington in 1968 and worked as a political analyst in the Bureau of Intelligence and Research. He then took Arab language training at the Foreign Service Institute in Beirut, followed by assignment as deputy principal *officer/commercial officer at Embassy Abu Dhab, United Arab Emirates.*

16
Lawrence W. I'Anson. *Retired Chief Justice of Virginia.* A lifelong resident, I'Anson began his legal career in Portsmouth in 1931. He served as commonwealth attorney from 1938 to 1941 and from 1941 to 1958 as judge in the Court of Hustings for the city of Portsmouth. In 1958 he became a member of the Supreme Court of Virginia and was named Chief Justice in 1974.

From 1979 to 1980, I'Anson served as president of the National Center for State Courts, as well as chairman of the National Conference of State Chief Justices.

He was chairman of the Virginia Court Systems Study Commission that recommended the reorganization of the state's courts, and the creation of an intermediate appellate court of appeals.

He served as chairman of the committee that wrote the Handbook for Jurors which is still used in all courts of record of Virginia.

I'Anson is currently the president and executive director of the Beazley Foundation, Inc., the city's largest private charitable trust.

17
G. Douglas Johnston. *Publisher of Vanity Fair magazine.* After spending five years in Louisville, Kentucky, selling radio advertising, Johnston made the transition to magazine advertising by joining Gentlemen's Quarterly in Chicago in 1976. He was named advertising director of the magazine in 1981.

In November 1981, Johnston joined the team laying the foundation for the renaissance of Vanity Fair. He was advertising director when he was named publisher in 1985.

18
Junius Kellogg. *Athlete. Exposed the national basketball fix scandal in the spring of 1951.*

Kellogg entered Manhattan College, where, as a basketball player, he was offered money by gamblers to "shave points" in an attempt to "fix" the score against DePaul University. Kellogg and his coach informed the authorities, after which Kellogg worked directly with the police until the "fixers" were apprehended. Through the efforts of Kellogg and Coach Ken Norton, the police were able to expose a basketball scandal which involved colleges across the country.

After graduation, Kellogg played for the Harlem Globetrotters. During the post-season barn-storming tour through Arkansas, Kellogg was involved in an auto accident, which left him paralyzed. After five years of rehabilitation in veterans' hospitals, he was hired as an accountant by Pan American World Airways.

While at Pan American, Kellogg coached its wheelchair sports team to five World Olympic Wheelchair Basketball championships, one national championship, and one runner-up in the national championship.

He is currently the first deputy commissioner of the New York City Community Development Agency.

19
Rear Adm. Herman Joseph Kossler. *During World War II, as commanding officer of the submarine Cavilla, Kossler led attacks on Japanese vessels that resulted in a South Pacific victory for the United States.* The submarine was involved in the sinking of the Japanese carrier Shokaku, home base for some of the planes that attacked Pearl Harbor.

Kossler's last active duty was as commandant of the Sixth Naval District in Charleston, South Carolina. Upon retirement in 1973, he was hired by the governor of South Carolina to build the Naval and Maritime Museum in Patriots Point. He retired from that position in 1978.

20
Frank D. Lawrence. *Banker and civic leader. Launched a career in baseball that brought him national acclaim.*

Lawrence organized his first baseball club in 1913 in the Old Virginia League and continued as the team's executive until the Piedmont League collapsed in 1955.

Lawrence sent many players to the major leagues, including Hall of Famer Pie Traynor and Hack Wilson, who became the National League's all-time home run king.

The Sporting News, a national baseball publication, recognized Lawrence as the Minor League Executive of 1943 after his Portsmouth club swept to the Piedmont League pennant. Lawrence is deceased.

21
Alf Johnson Mapp, Jr. *Author, historian. Eminent professor at Old Dominion University.*

Mapp has written more than eight hundred articles in the New York Times and other newspapers and scholarly journals and magazines. He is the author of documentary television and film scripts in the fields of American and English history. Mapp has written six books. The most recent, Thomas Jefferson: A Strange Case of Mistaken Identity, was a Book-of-the-Month Club selection in May 1987. His writings have circled the globe in nine languages.

Mapp is co-editor and adviser for nine books on American history and is cited as a reference source in Encyclopedia Britannica, Worldmark Encyclopedia, and World Book Encyclopedia.

He has received numerous national and international awards, and was nominated for a Pulitzer Prize in 1953. In 1981, in ceremonies in the State Capitol, he was made Commonwealth of Virginia Laureate. Mapp is included in twenty-eight encyclopedias and other reference works published in three nations. For a decade, he has consistently been one of a score of Virginians in Who's Who in the World.

22
Tommy Newsom. *Musician.* Assistant music director to Doc Severinsen on the "Tonight Show," serving as a full time arranger and part-time conductor. He has been with the show since 1962. He plays with jazz combos around the country and as a soloist with symphony orchestras.

Newsom has arranged and composed for Benny Goodman, Skitch Henderson, Woody Herman, Charlie Byrd, and Andre Kostelanetz. His most recent composition is "Air and Rondo" for alto saxophone and concert band.

Newsom has returned to his hometown many times during the years. In 1980, he was honored at "Tommy Newsom Day" and in 1986 he performed at the Seawall Festival with another former resident, Mahlon Clark, also a Portsmouth "Notable." He has performed locally with the Virginia Pops and at Old Dominion University. He recently received an honorary doctorate from Old Dominion University, where he was speaker for the 1987 commencement.

23

Dr. James Cuthbert Owens. *Nationally known surgeon, recognized for his work in trauma and emergency medical treatment. He is currently a professor at the University of Colorado Medical Center. He has published eighty-eight papers on related subjects.*

Between 1964 and 1979, he served on more than thirty state and national boards, commissions, and councils dealing with emergency care. He has participated in twenty-five audio-visual tapes for the "education of the rural physician in emergency care of the critically injured."

In 1985 he received the Valentine E. Wohlauer, M.D. award for Physicians' Excellence in Emergency Medical Surgery. The Colorado Medical Society awarded him the Certificate for Service for "Dedicated Educator and Communicator." He received the Trauma Achievement Award for exceptionally meritorious service as a member of a regional committee on trauma. He has been nominated for an award for the Most Significant Contribution to the Education of Minority Students.

24

Clarence "Ace" Parker. *Member of the Football Hall of Fame. While at Wilson High School he was a five-sports star and All-Tidewater football player in 1932.*

Parker was an All-American quarterback at Duke. He played professional football with the Brooklyn Dodgers before serving as a Navy lieutenant in World War II. Following the war, he played with the New York Yankees and was one of the best passers during a period when football was evolving from a ground-oriented game into the pass-punctuated one that it is today. He was named the most valuable player in the National Football League in 1940.

Parker also played professional baseball in the major leagues and hit a home run for the first time at bat for the Philadelphia Athletics.

In 1985, the Norfolk Sports club named him the Metropolitan Man of the Year in Sports. A member of the Pro Football Hall of Fame, he continues to serve as a scout for the St. Louis Cardinals.

25

William Schneider. *One of the country's leading political analysts. He is a resident fellow at the American Enterprise Institute in Washington, D.C., and a contributing editor to the* Los Angeles Times, *and* National Journal, Atlantic, *and* Public Opinion *magazines. He writes a weekly column, "Political Pulse," for the Los Angeles Times Syndicate.* Newsweek *recently referred to him as "the nation's hot new political pundit."*

Schneider is a frequent television guest expert and featured speaker on public affairs. His series of articles dealing with the 1987 election and American politics after Reagan, appeared in the Atlantic between January and July 1987. Schneider is co-author of The Confidence Gap: Business, Labor and Government in the Public Mind, *published in 1983 by the Free Press. A second edition was published in 1987.*

26

William B. Spong, Jr. *Former U.S. Senator from Virginia and former dean of the Marshall-Wythe School of Law at the College of William and Mary.*

Spong served in the U.S. Senate from 1967 to 1973 after a career in the Virginia House and Senate for twelve years.

Since retiring as dean of the Marshall-Wythe School of Law, Spong has taught at Washington and Lee University and the University of Virginia and attended the Institute for Advanced Legal Studies at the University of London. He has received honorary degrees from Hampden-Sydney College, Roanoke College, Washington and Lee University, and the College of William and Mary.

In 1985 he received the Virginia Chamber of Commerce Distinguished Service Award. He has served as president of the Virginia Bar Association and has held numerous other offices, including chairman of the Virginia Commission of Public Education and the chairman of the Commission of Virginia's Future. He is currently a member of the Virginia State Council of Higher Education and a trustee of the Virginia State Library Foundation.

27

Theodore Taylor. *Author of more than thirty adult non-fiction and children's books. His book* The Cay *was made into a movie in 1974, starring James Earl Jones. His latest book,* The Stalker, *is his first attempt at adult fiction. The suspense thriller will also be made into a movie.*

A former newspaper reporter who started as a sportswriter at the old Portsmouth Star, he has received fourteen literary awards for children's books. Taylor left Cradock at age seventeen to join the Washington, D.C. Daily News as a copy boy, living on eleven dollars a week. Two years later he was writing radio network sports for NBC in New York.

During World War II, Taylor served as a seaman on a gasoline tanker, later becoming a naval officer in the Pacific theater. He was recalled to active duty a few months after the Korean War began.

In 1955, a year after publication of his first book, The Magnificent Mitscher, *Taylor joined Paramount Pictures as a press agent and eventually worked himself up to associate producer. He also wrote, produced, and directed seventeen documentary films.*

28

Lt. Gen. William Gilbert Townsend Tuttle, Jr. *Deputy commanding general for logistics, U.S. Army Training and Doctrine Command, and commanding general of the U.S. Army Logistics Center at Fort Lee.*

His twenty-nine-year career has included service in Korea and Vietnam as a transportation officer, and in Europe in the 3rd Armored Division as assistant chief of staff, logistics; commander, 503rd Supply and Transport Battalion; and commander of the Division Support Command. In 1979 he was promoted to brigadier general and assigned as commanding general, Eastern Area Military Traffic Management Command.

General Tuttle has taught at West Point and served as director of force management for the Department of the Army in Washington; chief of the Policy and Programs Branch at Supreme Headquarters, Allied Powers Europe; and the commanding general, U.S. Army Operational Test and Evaluation Agency in Falls Church.

His awards and decorations include the Defense Superior Service Medal, the Legion of merit, and the Bronze Star. He is a 1958 graduate of West Point and holds an MBA from Harvard University.

bibliography

Andrews, Matthew Page. *Virginia the Old Dominion.* New York, 1937.

Benedict, David. *A General History of the Baptist Denominations in America.* Boston, 1813.

Bruce, Philip Alexander. *Economic History of Virginia in the Seventeenth Century.* Vols. I & II. New York, 1895-96.

Brydon, George MacLaren. *Virginia's Mother Church and the Political Conditions Under Which It Grew....1607-1727.* Richmond, 1947.

Burton, H. W. *The History of Norfolk Virginia: A review of Important Events and Incidents which occurred from 1736 to 1877; Also a Record of Personal Reminiscences and Political, Commercial, and Curious Facts.* Norfolk, Va. 1877.

Butt, Marshall W. *Portsmouth Under Four Flags: 1752-1970.* Portsmouth, Va., 1971.

_____. *Early Portsmouth Physicians: 1761-1906.* Portsmouth, Va., 1969.

Cross, Charles B. Jr. and Eleanor Phillips. *Chesapeake: A Pictorial History.* Norfolk, Va., 1985.

Dabney, Virginius. *Virginia the New Dominion.* Garden City, N.Y., 1971.

Daniel, J. R. V. (ed.). *A Hornbook of Virginia History.* Richmond, 1949.

Deans, Lelia A. *A Brief History of Public Education in Portsmouth.* Portsmouth, Va.: Privately Printed, 1964.

Eckenrode, H. J. *The Revolution in Virginia.* Boston and New York, 1916.

Edwards, Bertha Winborne (ed.). *Lee Rodgers Collection* (Pictures). 7 Vols. Compiled by Edwards for the Virginia Room of the Portsmouth Public Library, 1988.

_____. *Portsmouth's Black History.* 2 Vols. Written and compiled by Edwards for the Virginia Room of the Portsmouth Public Library, 1979.

Eller, Ernest McNeill (ed.). *Chesapeake Bay in the American Revolution.* Centreville, MD, 1981.

Emmerson, John C., Jr. *The Emmersons and Portsmouth, 1737-1965.* Portsmouth, Va.: Privately printed, 1966.

Flippin, Percy G. *Royal Government in Virginia, 1624-1775.* New York, 1919.

Gardner, Allen W. *A Naval History of the American Revolution.* Vols. I & II. New York, 1962.

Hallahan, John M. *The Battle of Craney Island.* Portsmouth, Va., 1986.

Hendren, Samuel Rivers. *Government and Religion of the Virginia Indians.* Baltimore, 1895.

Hobbs, Kermit and William A. Paquette. *Suffolk: A Pictorial History.* Norfolk, Va., 1987.

Holladay, Miss Mildred M. "A History of Portsmouth," in the *Portsmouth (Va.) Star,* January 19, 1936.

Johnson, Brooks. *Mountaineers to Main Streets.* Norfolk, Va., 1985.

Johnston, Henry P. *The Yorktown Campaign and the Surrender of Cornwallis, 1781.* New York, 1881.

Lamb, Robert W. (ed.). *Our Twin Cities of the Nineteenth Century.* Norfolk, Va., 1887-89.

Lossing, Benson J. *The Pictorial Field-Book of the Revolution.* Vol. II. Rutland, Vt., 1972. (originally published in 1859 by Harper & Brothers).

Mapp, Alf J., Jr. *The Virginia Experiment.* 3rd ed. New York and Lanham, Md., 1987.

Mays, David. *Edmund Pendleton.* Vols. I & II. Chapel Hill, N. C., 1960.

Moran, John L. *A History of Churchland Baptist Church: 1954-1981.* Privately printed, 1985.

Morton, Richard L. *Colonial Virginia.* Vols. I & II. Chapel Hill, N. C., 1960.

Norfolk Virginian, The. Illustrated Edition. Norfolk, Va., 1897.

Pollock, Edward. *Sketch Book of Portsmouth, Va. Its People and Its Trade.* Portsmouth, Va., 1886.

Porter, John W. H. *A Record of Events in Norfolk County, Virginia, From April 19th, 1861, to May 10th, 1862, with a History of the Soldiers and Sailors of Norfolk County, Norfolk City and Portsmouth Who served in the Confederate States Army or Navy.* Portsmouth, Va., 1892.

Quarles, Benjamin. *The Negro in the American Revolution.* Chapel Hill, N. C., 1961.

Squires, W. H. T. *Through the Years in Norfolk.* Portsmouth, Va., 1937.

State Historical Markers of Virginia. Bicentennial Edition. Richmond, Va., 1975.

Stewart, William H. *History of Norfolk County, Virginia and Representative Citizens.* Chicago, 1902.

Vaché, Rev. Charles C. *A History of Trinity Church: Portsmouth Parish.* Portsmouth, Va., 1962.

Virginia Writers' Project. *The Negro in Virginia*. New York, 1940.

Virginian-Pilot/Ledger-Star, Norfolk, Va., various issues.

Ward, Christopher. *The War of the Revolution*. Vols. I & II. New York, 1952.

Wentz, Robert W., Jr. *Portsmouth: A Pictorial History*. Norfolk, Va., 1975.

Wertenbaker, Thomas J. *Norfolk: Historic Southern Port*. Durham, N. C., 1931, 2nd ed. edited by Marvin W. Schlegel, 1962.

——— *Torchbearer of the Revolution: The Story of Bacon's Rebellion and Its Leader*. Princeton, 1940.

index

A
A & N Stores, 158
Accomac County, 15, 98
Adair, Rear Adm. Jamie, 161
Adams, Dr. Mac Carter, 217, 219
Adder (Submarine), 93
AFL-CIO, 206
Agee, Kenneth A., 75
Alabama, 98
Albertson, Mrs. Robert B., 200
Alexander Park, 174
Alexandria, 11, 13, 15, 108
Alf J. Mapp Junior High School, 68, 71
Alford, Dr. M. E., 69, 188
Algonquins, 19
All-America City, 11, 198, 200, 215
Allen, Rear Adm. Edward C., Jr., 176, 217, 219
American Institute of Architects, 11
American National Bank, 183
Andarton, William, 155
Anderson, Harold B., 111
Andrews, Virginia C., 217, 219
Ann Street School. *See* John Marshall
Ansel, W. Guy, 111
Anthony, E., 130
Appomattox, 104
Arkansas, 98
Armantrout, 130
Armistead house, 211
Armistead, Rev. Thomas, 34
Armory, 152
Armstrong, G., 114
Arnold, Brig. Gen. Benedict, 46, 47
Arthur Murray Dance Studio, 183
Ashton, John C., 63
Atlantic Coast Line, 166
Atlantic and Danville Railroad, 113, 166
Averitt, Joseph, 80
Ayres Seafood, 133

B
B. H. Owens', Staple and Fancy Dry Goods, 115
Bacon, Nathaniel, 22, 25
Bacon's Rebellion, 22, 25
Bacot, George, 168
Bain, R. T. K., 119
Bain, T. A., 130
Bain, Winston, 190
Baird, J. Thompson, 198
Baker, Barnabas W. (Billy), 10, 41, 198
Baker, E. L. (Buck), 168
Baker, William Hodges, 130
Baliles, Gov. Gerald L., 207, 215
Baltimore, 78, 107, 108, 209
Bangel, Herbert K., 161
Baptist General Association of Virginia, 60
Baptist World Alliance, 35
Barbary States, 52
Barnes, Jack P., 9, 167, 195, 198, 203
Barnes, Richard E. (Dick), 9, 79
Barron, Commodore James, 35, 55, 56, 57, 216
Bartlett, A. C., 198
Bart Street, 130
Basket manufacturing, 124
Bates, W. B., 111
Bayston, Beverly, 58
Bayview Boulevard, 212
Beazley family, 216
Beazley, Frederick W., 84, 85, 161
Beckwith, Brig. Gen. Sir Sidney, 55
Bellamy Foundation, 203
Beltline, 164
Belton, Philip, 81
Benjamin Franklin (merchant ship), 97
Bennett's Creek Road, 35
Benton, Fire Chief Odell, 9, 157
Bergeron, City Engineer, 163
Berkeley, Gov. Sir William, 20, 22, 24, 25
Berkeley Hundred, 21
Berkeley Bridge, 174
Berkley, 52, 98, 109
Berkley (ferry), 182
Bicentennial, National, 11, 81, 179, 202
Bilisoly, Antonio S. (1759-1845), 46
Bilisoly, Dr. Antonio, 111, 119
Black Hawk, Chief, 8, 11, 87
Black Patti (Sissieretta Jones), 118
Blacks, 20, 21, 97
Blondo, Petty Officer Steve, 9
Board of Architectural Review, 200
Board of Health, 119
Bond, Margaret, 83
Bonhomme Richard (ship), 42, 46
Booth, J. W., 130
Boster, Ben, Sr., 9
Boston, 78
Boutakoff, Rear Admiral, 107
Braddock, Maj. Gen. Edward, 43
Brady, Mathew, 105
Brennaman, Marty, 217, 219
Briggs School, 65
Bristol-built houses, 12, 112, 210
Britain, 104, 131
British Army, 43
British Navy, 26, 43, 44, 45, 46
Brockwell, Sherwood, 157
Broke, Capt. P. B. V., 56
Brooks, Dr. Vernon A., 198
Broughton, Police Chief J. M., 155
Brown, Ruth Weston, 217, 219
Brown, the Right Reverend William Ambrose, 153, 161
Brown, William A. III, 9
Brown v. Board of Education, 177
Bruce, Billie, 168
Bruckner, Robert H., 217, 219
Buchanan, President James, 87
Bunting, Mary Tom, 80
Burgess, Dean, 9
Burton, Susan, 9
Butler, Maj. Gen. Benjamin F., 102, 104
Butt, Marshall W., Jr., 9
Butt, Marshall W., Sr., 26, 31, 173, 179, 181, 186
Byrd Anti-lynch Law, 147
Byrd, Harry Flood, 147
Byrd, Richard E., 152

C
Cadmus, Lt. C. L., 155
Calvert, Lewis, 155
Campbell, Dr. Robert M., 161
Canadaigua, USS, 92
Canby, Gen., 198
Candle, The, 179
Caribbean, 46
Carney, Barnaby, 31
Carney family, 216
Carney, James H., 59
Carney, Richard, 31, 58
Carney, Capt. Stephen (1810-1890), 213
Carney, Stephen Barnaby, 124
Carney, Wright Bruce, 124
Carolinas, 45
Carr, Dr. George, 110, 128
Carrie B. (harbor tour boat), 203, 204
Carver, Capt. William, 24, 25
Cassell family, 210
Cassell House, 210
Cassell, V. O., 119
Cavalier Manor, 212
Cedar Lane, 36
Centenary Methodist Church, 36
Central Methodist Church, 37
Cervera, Adm. Pascual, 110
Chamber of Commerce, Junior, 157
Chamber of Commerce, Portsmouth, 9, 163, 169, 188, 201
Chambers Fire Company, 154, 157
Chambers Hook and Ladder Company, 154
Chanco, 22
Channel, Gale Atwood, 9
Channel, Mary Brown, 9, 10, 38
Chapman, R. W., 111
Chapman, William, 130
Chapman's Jewelers, 111
Charleston, 11
Chatauqua Avenue, 147
Cherry, Arthur Lee, 161
Cherry, Bradford L., 161
Cherry, Dr. T. Mack, 82
Chesapeake, USS, 50, 52, 54, 55, 56, 57, 92
Chesapeake Bay, 15, 19, 25, 55, 108, 209
Chesapeake, city, 13, 14, 15, 19, 20, 22, 84, 174
Chesapeake Female College, 60
Chesapeakes (Indians), 20
Chestnut Street, 61, 117, 118, 131
Chestnut Street School, 61
Chicago, 108
Children's Museum, 88, 200, 205
Chrysler Museum, 10
Churches. *See* individual names
Churchill, Ora, 81
Churchland, 35, 36, 39, 59, 78, 124, 125, 169, 174, 186, 187, 201, 213
Churchland Academy, 59
Churchland Baptist Church, 35
Churchland High School, 78, 82
Circle Restaurant, 183
Citizen's Trust (now Signet) Building, 185, 188
City Council, 119, 195, 199, 200
City Hall, 108, 129
City Managers, 111
City Market, 152
City of Portsmouth (ferry), 180
City Park, 49, 129, 139, 186
Civic Center, 167, 195, 198, 203
Civil War, 22, 28, 34, 58, 92, 93, 98, 99, 102, 105, 107, 111, 147, 210
Clark, Mahlon, 217, 219
Clarke, S. J., 77
Clarke Junior High School, 77
Clay, Henry, 8, 11
Claytor, Graham, 167
Clements, E. D., 130
Cleveland, President Grover, 112
Cleveland, Rev. Richard, 112, 119
Clifford Street, 118
Clinton, Sir Henry, 46
Coast Guard, 9, 175, 176, 199, 200
Coast Guard Lightship Museum, 176, 188, 200, 206
Codd, J. Leon, 64, 65
Cogentrix steam-generating plant, 216
Coleman's Nursery, 204
Collier, Commodore Sir George, 45

225

Colliers, Cary, 112
Collins, Daniel, 198
Collins, Margaret, 32
Colony Theater, 131
"Colored Notes," 163
Columbia Street, 62
Columbian Exposition, World's, 108
Commerce Park, 216
Commercial Place, Norfolk, 174
Committee of Safety, 44, 45
Commodore Theater, 121, 216
Community Arts Center, 200
Company F, First Regiment, Virginia Foot, 88
Concord Wharf, 108
Confederate forces, 100, 102, 103, 104, 105, 107, 110, 111
Confederate Monument, 129, 193
Congress, U.S., 21, 52, 55
Congress, USS, 102
Connecticut, 21
Constellation (frigate), 52, 55
Constitution (frigate), 52
Continental Army, 44, 46
Continental Congress at Philadelphia, 44, 45, 88
Conway, Capt. (Ret.) Theodore, 9
Cooke Street School. *See* John Marshall School
Cornwallis, Gen. Lord, 45, 46, 47, 200, 202
Cossack Street (later Portsmouth Boulevard), 107
County Street, 26, 122
Court House, 1803, 88
Court House, 1846, 35, 53, 88, 97, 119, 131, 179, 182, 200, 207
Court House Gallery, 200
Court Street, 12, 16, 26, 30, 33, 34, 88, 108, 117, 129, 130, 131, 132, 141, 142, 145, 149, 172, 179, 183, 190, 193, 197, 200, 205, 206, 210, 215
Court Street Baptist Church, 9, 34, 52, 53, 60, 119, 129
Cowan, Ralph W., 217
Cox, Capt. John, 46
Cox, Dr. & Mrs. Russell M., 210
Cox, Dr. Russell M., 161
Crab Street, 26
Cradock, Rear Adm. Sir Christopher George Francis Maurice, 136
Cradock, 135, 136, 159, 174, 222
Cradock bandstand, 204
Cradock Elementary School, 71
Cradock Fire Station, 156
Cradock High School, 71
Craft, Hinton, 168

Craney Island, 55, 98, 103, 105, 113, 174
Craney Island School, 59
Crawford, Col. William, 17, 25, 26, 28, 29, 31, 52, 179, 197
Crawford House, 87
Crawford Street (Parkway), 8, 26, 28, 46, 47, 49, 51, 58, 59, 108, 112, 114, 117, 122, 129, 150, 152, 175, 178, 183, 184, 193, 210
Creech, Thomas, 31
Creech's Jewelers, 179
CRESTAR (formerly United Virginia Bank), 168
Crocker, Maj. James Francis, 60
Cross, Eleanor Phillips, 9
Crozet, Col. Claude, 87
Cuba, 110
Culpepper, D. P., 155
Cumberland, USS, 102

D
Dabney, Virginius, 102
Dale, Commodore Richard, 42, 46, 48, 50, 52
Davis, Jefferson, 102
Davis, Lt. Gov. Richard J., 9, 161, 195, 196, 198, 217, 218, 220
Davis, L. H., 198
Davis, William J., Palace Stable, 121
Deans, Capt. John E., 97
Deans, Capt. John N., 100
Deans, William, 111
Decatur, Commodore Stephen, 57
Declaration of Independence, 22, 45
Delaware (ship), 86, 87, 179
Deltaville, 108
Depression, 148, 159
DeVere, Louise, 9
Dewey, Adm. George, 110
Dick, Lacy W., 10
Diggs, Jessie, 155
Diggs, William, 155
Dillsburg, William, 155
Dinks, Marshall, 168
Dinwiddie Street, 33, 133, 192, 209
Dismal Swamp, 19
Dominion Bank, 124
Doolittle, Mrs. James H., 162
Downtown Merchants Association, 200, 205
Downtown Tunnel, 180
Duke, Fred A., 198
Duke of Kent, 162
Duncan, Daniel W., 161
Dunmore, John Murray, earl of, 43, 44, 45
Dunne, Ray J. 163, 169

E
Earls, Dr. Julian M. 218, 220
Early, E. Saunders, Jr., 161, 195
Eastern Shore, Maryland, 15, 25
Eastern Shore, Virginia, 13, 14, 15, 20, 22, 108. *See* also Accomac County and Northampton County
Eastes, George D., 161
Ebenezer Baptist Church, 40
Ebenezer Plaza, 40
Eckstine, Allen M., 9, 75
Edwards, A. T., 76
Edwards, Bertha Winborne, 9, 163
Edwards, Maj. Griffin F., 62
Edwards, Dr. Rondle E., 82
Effingham Street, 33, 37, 157
Elizabeth City County, 22, 98
Elizabeth Manor, 174, 213
Elizabeth River, 15, 20, 22, 25, 26, 43, 44, 87, 103, 107, 108, 173, 175, 180, 190, 191, 192, 204, 212, 213
Elizabeth River Parish, 31
Elks, 211
Ellis, H. Perry, 218, 220
Emancipation Proclamation, 98
Embargo Act, 55
Emmanuel African Methodist Episcopal Church, 37
Emmerson, Capt. Arthur, 55, 87, 90
Emmerson, J. Cloyd, 9, 181, 183
Emmerson family, 121
Emurian, Rev. Ernest K., 161
English basement houses, 12, 112, 210
Eppling, Nancy, 79
Etheredge & Brooks, Cotton Factors and General Commission Merchants, 114
Etheridge, Amos, 197
Etz, Betty, 9
Eustis, Peter, 161
Ewell, George T., 161

F
Famous, The, 80, 131, 179
Fass, Isaac Seafood, 147, 183
Fass, Sol, 161
Federal Building, 175, 179
Federal forces, 34, 100, 102, 103, 104, 105, 107
Federal Government, 58, 92, 97, 98, 174
Federal occupation, 28, 33
Ferebee, John, 31
Ferguson Drive, 213
Ferries, 11, 22, 87, 117, 151, 173, 174, 181, 183, 190, 196, 204
Fifth Coast Guard District, 9, 199, 200

Fifth Ward School. *See* John Marshall School
Fillmore, President Millard, 87
First Methodist Society, 33
First Presbyterian Church, 31, 33, 112, 119, 182
First Street, 138, 176
Fiske, D. D., 197
Fleming, P. Stockton, 161
Flora, William, 44
Florida, 98
Florida (Old Bay Line steamer), 126
Fontaine, Louise N., 185
Fort Lane, 143, 175
Fort Lee, 222
Fort Monroe, 102, 104
Fort Nelson, 45, 89
Fourth Street, 160, 197
Fourth Virginia Regiment, 45, 46
Fox, Leslie T., 161, 198
Franklin, USS, 106
Frederick College, 69, 84
Frederick Military Academy, 84, 85
Frederick W. Beazley Foundation, 84
Fredericksburg, 13, 15
Freedom Train, 166
Freeman, Reverend Mr., 58
Freeze, James T., 161
Fremont, Gen. John Charles, 98
French, Floyd, 140
French, 43, 46, 52, 55, 104, 131, 134
French Bakery, 215
French and Indian War, 43
Fry, Leslie L., 203

G
G. Armstrong & Son, Saw and Planing Mill, 114
G. Weinberg, Inc.: Lockers/Naval Outfitters, 152
Gardner, Alexander, 105
Gardner, James, 105
Garrett, B. Jane, 9, 217
Gaskins, D. V., 115
Gaskins & Sturtevant, Funeral Directors and Embalmers, 115
Gates Theater, 179
Ge Qiyun, 207
General Assembly, 21, 26, 31, 46, 47, 51, 88
George L. Neville, Wholesale and Retail Dealer, 114
Georgetown, 11
Georgia, 98
Gilbert, Thomas, 25
Gill, Bruce Murdaugh, 9
Gill, Franklin D. & Cora Mapp, 120
Gill House, 120
Glasgow Street, 13, 16

226

Glasgow Street Academy, 58, 62, 210, 211
Glasgow Street Female School, 61
Glasgow Street Male School, 61
Glensheallah, 212
Glover, David C., 217, 218, 220
Gluse, Shelley L., 9
Godspeed (ship), 21
Goldblatt, Abe, 217
Gomley Chesed Synagogue, 37, 39
Gosport, 26, 27, 44, 45, 51, 52, 55, 87, 92, 204
Gosport (steam ferry), 87
Grand Dukes Alexis and Constantine, 107, 162
Grange Hall, 124
Grant, David M., 157
Grant, Jordan Winslow, 157
Grant, Gen. Ulysses, 99
Grasse, de, Admiral, 46
Grayson Street, 209
Great Bridge, 84, 174
Great Britain, 55
Great White Fleet, 110
"Green Spring" mansion, 20
Green Street, 37, 62, 108
Green Street School, 61
Green, J. H., 129
Greyhound bus terminal, 158
Grice, George W., 197
Griffin, Diane, 9
Griffin, John T., Mr. & Mrs., 124
Griffith, Virginia, 73
Grimes Battery, 55, 135, 137, 138, 139
Grimes, Capt. Cary F., 100
Grimes, Thomas, 31
Gwynn's Island, 45
Gygax, Rear Adm. Felix, 161

H
Haile, Peggy, 10
Hall, Harry C., 155
Hall, Florence, 74
Hall, James E., 9
Hamby, Ramona, 109
Hamilton, U.S. Rep. Norman, 153, 161
Hamilton (Old Dominion steamer), 126
Hampton Boulevard, Norfolk, 175
Hampton, city, 13, 15, 45, 201, 215
Hampton Roads, 13, 14, 15, 19, 20, 22, 44, 45, 46, 55, 97, 98, 100, 103, 107, 108, 110, 131, 136, 147, 159, 201, 215, 216
Hampton Roads Anglo-American Friendship Day, 200
Han Nu, Ambassador, Peoples Republic of China, 207
Hanbury, George L. II, 111, 187, 201, 206
Hanbury, John Paul C., 10, 161, 200
Hanes, Alice C., 9, 217
Hanger, S. T., 130
Hannay, Sir David, 206
Hanrahan, Frank C., 111
Hanvey, James T., 198
Harbor Court Hotel, 145
Harbor Tower, 184, 216
Hardy, U.S. Rep. Porter, Jr., 9, 161, 187, 188, 189
Hardy, Mrs. Porter, Jr., 187
Hargroves, Reverend Dr. Carney, 35
Harper, Chandler, 168, 217, 218, 220
Harper, Charles F., 111
Harper's Ferry, 97, 98
Harriet Lane (U.S. Revenue Cutter), 100
Harris, Charles F., 218, 220
Harry A. Hunt Junior High School, 64, 66
Hatcher, Catherine, 10
Hatton, Alex, 140
Hatton, Goodrich, 119
Hatton Street, 211
Haug, M. E., 111
Hawks, Edward B., 111
Helping Hands Mission, 160
Henry VIII, 205
Herbert, John, 31
High Street, 11, 13, 26, 30, 37, 46, 47, 49, 51, 52, 53, 65, 88, 90, 112, 114, 115, 116, 117, 121, 122, 126, 128, 129, 130, 131, 144, 149, 150, 151, 157, 158, 172, 174, 179, 182, 186, 187, 190, 195, 200, 201, 207, 211, 214, 216
Hill, Abner B., 161
Hill, Collins, 168
Hill, Dorothy M., 9
Hill, Evelyn & Lizzie, 185
Hill House, 185
Hinton, A. C., 9
Historic District, 200
Historical Markers, 30
Hodges, Col. James G., 100, 197
Hodges, John, 58
Hofheimer, B. F., 130
Hoggard, Thurmer, 58
Holiday Inn, 184, 188
Holiday Inn Marina, 206
Holladay, James G., 98
Holladay, Mildred, 9, 42
Holley, Dr. James W. III, 198, 199
Holmes, Rufae J., 77
Hope, F. S., 198
Horton, Phineas, 111
Horwege, Richard A., 6, 105, 128
Hospital Point, 44, 45, 126, 132, 173
House, G. Robert, 203
House, Mrs. G. Robert, 9
House of Burgesses, 21, 25, 43
House of Delegates, 64
Howard, Rear Adm. W. F., Jr., 186
Howell, W. Nathaniel, 218, 220
Howlett's Photography, 112
Hudgins, Bilisoly, 168
Hume, Jimmie, 168
Hume, Rev. Thomas, 60
Hume, Tom, 168
Hunt, Harry, 64, 75, 161
Hunt, John, 154
Hunter's Lane, 132
Hutchins, R. A., Jr., 198

I
I. C. Norcom High School, 61, 68, 69, 70, 76, 77, 78, 83
I'Anson, Chief Justice Lawrence W., 10, 161, 217, 218, 221
Idaho (battleship), 148
Illustrious, HMS (British aircraft carrier), 162
International Association of Police Chiefs, 155
Irish row house, 210
Isle of Wight County, 187
Ives, James, 31

J
J. & E. Mahoney, Rectifier and Wholesale Liquor Dealers, 121
Jackson, President Andrew, 8, 11, 25, 87
Jackson, Thomas J. (Stonewall), 104
Jackson Ward, 197
Jakeman, E. F., 111
James River, 15, 19, 21, 22, 46, 84, 102, 215
James River Bridge, 215
Jamestown, 20, 21, 22, 43
Jamestown Colony, 19
Jamestown Exposition, 110, 128, 135, 145
Jarvis, A. B., 130
Jefferson, President Thomas, 45, 55
Jefferson Ward, 197
Jervey, J. P., 111
Johansen, Rear Adm. Julian E. (Joe), 9, 176, 198, 199, 204
John Marshall School, 63, 64, 72, 73, 74, 75
Johnson, Anthony, 21
Johnson, Aubrey P., Jr., 111, 186
Johnson, Brooks, 10
Johnson, Dr. Harvey N., Jr., 9
Johnson, the Reverend Dr. Harvey N., Sr., 40, 177
Johnson, President Lyndon B., 177
Johnston, G. Douglas, 218, 221
Jones, Capt. Catesby ap R., 98
Jones, John Paul, 42, 46
Jones, Matilda Sissieretta Joyner, 118
Jones, Pamela, 9
Jordan, Ida Kay, 9
Jupiter (collier), 135, 140

K
Kellogg, Junius, 171, 218, 221
Kennedy, President John F., 177
King Street, 13, 26, 63, 65, 112
King's Daughters Hospital, 142, 143
Kingman, Mrs. Josepha, 124
Kirby, Frank L., 161
Kirn, Henry, 124, 151
Kirn Building, new, 124, 151, 179
Kirn Building, old, 115, 124
Kirn Hall, 124
Kirn Memorial Library, Norfolk, 124
Kise, Dr. Merl A., 161
Kissinger, Secretary of State Henry, 195
School Board, 119, 199
Kittery, Maine, 92
Knight, Lester Lloyd, 161
Knights of Columbus, 37
Kossler, Rear Adm. Herman J., 218, 221
Kron Prinz Wilhelm (German sea raider), 135
Ku Klux Klan, 147

L
Lafayette, James, 46, 47
Lafayette, Marquis de, 8, 11, 46, 47, 49, 87, 162
Lafayette Memorial Arch, 183, 200, 202
Lafayette Park, 183
Lancaster, Prof. A. J., 79, 161
Land, William, 155
Langley, USS, 92, 135, 140
Larkin, George, 140
Law, Joe M., 9
Lawrence, Frank W., 161, 218, 221
Lawrence, Capt. James, 55, 56
Lawrence, John O., 198
Lawrence, Maywood O., 161
Lawrence, T. S., 130
Ladies Professional Golf Association Tournament, 169
Ledger-Dispatch, 175
Ledger-Star, 121
Lee, Gen. Charles, 44, 45
Lee, Gov. Fitzhugh, 110

Lee, Richard Henry, 45
Lee, Robert E., 11, 98, 104, 107, 109, 110
Leigh, Doris S., 170
Leigh, John P., 198
Leigh, Dr. William, 210
Leopard (British frigate), 55, 57
Letcher, Gov. John, 98, 100
Levy, Nathan, 130
Lexington (carrier), 95
Lighthouse Service, 176
Lincoln, President Abraham, 98, 102
Lincolnsville, 175
Lively, Charles, 182
London Boulevard (Street), 16, 26, 28, 29, 33, 179, 206, 210
Long, Anne Hyde, 161
Long, Richard, 9
Lossing, Benson John, 47
Louisiana, 98
Luray (Old Dominion Line steamer), 126

M
MacKenzie, Judge John A., 161
Macklin, Dr. A. G., 77
MacMurran, Judge Robert, 41
Macon House, 87
Madison Street, 107
Magann, Wilfred F., 161
Magnien, Col. Bernard, 46, 56
Mahoney, J. & E., Rectifier and Wholesale Liquor Dealers, 121
Majette, Mary Norcom, 70
Mallory, Stephen R., 102
Maloney, William J., 9
Mapp Act, 121
Mapp, Alf J., Jr., 205, 217, 218, 221
Mapp, Alf J., Sr., 68, 75, 77, 177
Marin, Alfred F., 9
Marion Rifles, 100
Market house, 211
Mary Rose Traveling Exhibit, 200, 205
Maryland, 14, 15, 176
Maryview Hospital, 142, 144
Massachusetts, 56
Mathew, Brig. Gen. Edward, 45
Mathews, Maj. Thomas, 45
Maupin, Brooke Butt, 9, 10
Maupin, Eddie Sam, 190
Maupin, Edward W., Jr., 161
Maupin, W., Jr., 130
Mayors, 197-198
Max, The, 167
Mayhall, Rev. Ruth, 39
McGavock, Martha, 80
McGinley, Charles, 111
McIntyre, Reba, 79

McLean, Amelia, 169, 186
McLean, George T., 161, 169, 186
McLean, Jean, 169
McRae, Capt. John W., 210
Mediterranean Squadron, 46
Melton, Dr. Nancy, 9, 205
Merchants' and Farmers' Bank, 124, 125
Merrimac. See *Virginia*, CSS
Merry Point, 108
Mexican War, 91, 97
Mexico, 88
Middle Peninsula, 13, 14, 15
Middle Street, 8, 26, 33, 46, 58, 112, 120, 122, 123, 124, 153, 179, 210
Middle Street Presbyterian Church, 33
Midtown Tunnel, 175
Miller, Andrew, 203
Miller, Dr. Margaret, 203
Miller, Francis, 197
Milligan House, 119
Milliner, Jack, 9
Mississippi (battleship), 148
Mississippi, 98, 147
Missouri, 98
Monitor, USS, 11, 93, 96, 102, 103, 105
Monongahela, 43
Monroe Hotel, 148, 149, 175
Monumental Methodist Church, 33, 131, 172
Moody, Sen. Willard J., 9, 189
Mook, Lt. Dennis, 9
Moonyah Club, 140
Morris, Guy, 9
Morris, John A., 130, 161
Mountbatten, Lord Louis, 162
Mt. Herman Baptist Temple, 31
Mt. Hermon, 195
Municipal Building, 1912, 53
Murdaugh, Claudius, 120
Murdaugh house, 28
Murdaugh, J. A., 140
Murray, Sgt. J. R., 9
Muscovite Street (later Madison Street), 107
Museum, Children's, 88, 200, 205
Museum, Chrysler, 10
Museum, Naval Shipyard, 9, 109, 179, 186
Museums, Portsmouth, 9, 88, 188, 200, 205
Museums and Fine Arts Commission, 205

N
Nansemond County, 187
Nansemond River, 15

Nansemonds, 20
Napoleon, 55
Nash family, 179
Nash, John, 198
National Grays, 97
National League of Municipalities, 200
National Municipal League, 110
National Music Council, 118
National Printing Company, 131
Naval Hospital, Portsmouth, 9, 89, 108, 110, 133, 136, 139, 142, 173, 175
Naval Place, 142
Naval Shipyard Museum, 9, 109 179, 186, 200
Navigation Acts, 51
Navy, U.S., 54, 87, 95, 100, 102, 108
Navy Yard, 11, 42, 43, 50, 76, 86, 89, 92, 93, 94, 95, 97, 99, 100, 102, 103, 104, 105, 107, 108, 109, 110, 127, 135, 137, 140, 147, 148, 152, 156, 159, 160, 162, 173, 174, 175, 179, 180, 184, 186, 190, 195, 200, 216
Neely, Johnson, 168
Negroes. See Blacks
Neville, Gen. Wendell Cushing, 134, 138
New Norfolk County. See Norfolk County
New Orleans, 13, 16, 98, 102
Newport News, 13, 14, 15, 45, 201, 215
New York, 44, 45, 46, 78, 97, 126
Newsom, Tommy, 218, 221
Newtown Academy, 61
Niemeyer, Tony, 140
Niemeyer, W. C., 140
Nimmo, Gershom, 26
Nina (ship), 108
Nivision-Ball-Albertson House, 8
Nix, John T., 161, 167
Nixon, President Richard M., 195
Norcom, Lt. Col. Henry Charles, 70
Norcom, I. C., 70
Norcom, James G., 9
Norcom, James G., Jr., 70
Norfolk (city), 13, 15, 22, 26, 31, 44, 45, 51, 52, 97, 98, 100, 102, 103, 104, 107, 108, 109, 121, 124, 136, 173, 174, 175, 180, 183, 187, 190, 194, 199, 201, 204, 205, 215
Norfolk County (also New Norfolk County), 22, 25, 31, 44, 52, 53, 87, 88, 97, 98, 100, 107, 110, 119, 121, 124, 125, 173, 174, 178, 180, 184, 187
Norfolk County Jail, 155, 191

Norfolk Naval Base, 110, 135
Norfolk Naval Shipyard. See Navy Yard
Norfolk and Portsmouth Baptist Church, 34
Norfolk Virginian, 121
North Carolina, 13, 14, 15, 46, 59, 102, 131, 157, 159, 160, 176
North Street, 8, 26, 37, 108, 141, 175, 178, 185, 210
Northampton County, 15, 21, 98
Northern Neck, 13, 14, 15
Nott, the Right Reverend Monsignor F. Harold, 161

O
O'Connor, John, 198
O'Rourke family, 179
Oast, Edward L., Jr., 195
Oast, William, 140
Ocean House, 87, 90, 117, 129, 131, 148, 175, 209
Old Bay Line, 126
Old Dominion, 88
Old Dominion Guard, 100
Old Dominion Line, 126
Old fish market, 121
Old Point, 46
Olde Towne, 200, 201, 209-211
Onley, Asst. Police Chief A. H., 155
Opecancanough, 22
Orton, Audrey, 9, 77
Orton, Vernon, 77
Orton, Wayne, 77
Outland, Rufus, 85
Owens, Arthur S., 111
Owens, B. H., 115
Owens, Dr. James C., 218, 222
Owens, Capt. John C., 100

P
Paradise Creek, 137
Parrish Memorial Hospital, 145
Park Manor, 74
Park Road, 212
Park View, 74, 132, 211
Park View Elementary school, 75
Parker, Clarence (Ace), 170, 217, 218, 222
Parker, Herman, 182
Parker, Col. Josiah, 46
Parker, Paul W., Jr., 9
Parker, Virgil, 182
Parliament, British, 21
Partridge, Capt. Alden, 87
Pass House, 28
Patti, Adelina, 118
Peabody Elementary School, 70
Peabody, Raymond A., 217

Pegram, Capt. Robert B., 98, 100
Peninsula, 14, 15
Pennington Drive, 212
Pennsylvania (ship), 99
Pershing, Gen. John J., 135, 137
Peters, John E., 10
Petersburg, 46
Philadelphia, 26, 60, 97
Phillips & Nash, Dry Goods and Notions, 115
Phillips, Maj. Gen. William, 46
Pierce, Barbara, 9
Pig Point Battery, 100
Pilgrims, 21
Pinners Point, 133, 151, 166, 175
Pinners Point Elementary School, 66
Pinta (ship), 108
Pittman, Sheila P., 217
Pittsburg, 43
Plymouth, USS, 92
Plymouth Rock, 21
Pociask, Joseph, 9
Pokey Smokey (steam engine), 186
Police Commissioners, 119
Polk, President James K., 87
Pollard, Gov. John Garland, 152
Port Centre, 216
Port Norfolk, 147, 150, 212
Port Norfolk Electric Railway Company, 150
Port Norfolk Elementary School, 65
Porter, John L., 102, 104
Portside, 194, 199
Portsmouth (Coast Guard ship), 176, 188, 200, 206
Portsmouth, England, 13, 26
Portsmouth, New Hampshire, 92
Portsmouth Academy, 58, 59, 87, 210
Portsmouth Advocate, 88
Portsmouth Assembly, 124
Portsmouth Basket Works, 108
Portsmouth Boat Club, 132
Portsmouth Boulevard, 107
Portsmouth City Planning Office, 10
Portsmouth General Hospital, 142, 143
Portsmouth General School of Nursing, 143
Portsmouth High School, 63, 64, 65, 76
Portsmouth Historical Foundation, 200
Portsmouth Insurance Company, 60
Portsmouth International Terminals, 167
Portsmouth Jail, 191
Portsmouth Juniors Football Team, 168

Portsmouth Light Artillery, 100
Portsmouth Marine Terminal, 66, 175
Portsmouth Museums, 9, 88, 188, 205
Portsmouth National Notables, 168, 169, 217
Portsmouth Notables Committee, 217
Portsmouth Parish, 30, 31, 46
Portsmouth Parish Glebe, 45
Portsmouth Police Department, 154, 155, 207
Portsmouth Pride, 201
Portsmouth Public Library, 119, 163
Portsmouth Republican and Virginia Commercial Gazette, 87-88
Portsmouth Retail merchants Association, 130
Portsmouth Rifles, 100
Portsmouth and Roanoke Railroad, 87, 167, 175
Portsmouth Savings Society, 87
Portsmouth Service League, 168
Portsmouth Sisters of Mercy, 100
Portsmouth Star, 121, 126, 146, 157, 158, 163, 175, 222
Portsmouth Street Railway, 107
Post Office, 117, 129, 130
Potomac River, 13, 15, 19
Powhatan, Indian Emperor, 19, 20, 22, 23
Powhatans, 19, 22
Prentis Park School, 64
Prentis Place, 110
Prince Oblinski, 107
Prince of Wales, 205
Princess Anne County, 25, 98, 187
Prinz Eitel Friederich (German sea raider), 135
Purcell, David, 197
Pythian Castle, 215

Q
Quality Shop, 187
Queen Street, 13, 26, 33, 34, 174, 179

R
Railroads, 60, 87, 107, 126, 164, 165, 166, 167, 175, 178, 191
Raleigh, USS, 108
Ramsbotham, Sir Peter, 200
Randolph, Giles, 31
Randolph Street, 138, 176
Rapoport, Herman, 187
Rapoport, Morris, 187
Rapoport, Reed, 9, 187

Rappahannock River, 15, 19
Red Lion Tavern, 29
Reed, J. Davis, 198
Reed, Robert M., 161
Reed, Dr. Walter, 97
Reed House, 29
Reina Mercedes (Spanish cruiser), 110
Resolution Fire Company, 154
Revolution, American, 9, 42, 43, 51, 92
Richardson, Harry, 132
Richardson, Ira J., 9
Richmond, 13, 15, 46, 98, 174, 175
Riddick-Weaver Elementary School, 70
Rivin, Zelma Goodman, 9, 80
Roanoke Island, 102
Robb, Gov. Charles, 205
Roberts, Humphrey, 197
Roberts, Rice, 76
Robertson, W. F., 130
Robinson, Jean, 80
Rodman, J. Roy, 161
Roe, James, 197
Rogers, Lee F., 163
Rolin and Keily's 1851 Map of Portsmouth, 17, 91
Roosevelt, President Franklin D., 11, 146, 148, 159, 162
Roosevelt, President Theodore, 11, 110, 128, 130
Rough Riders, 110
Rowland, Robert G., 169
Royal Navy. *See* British Navy

S
St. Helena Division of College of William and Mary, 68
St. John's Episcopal Church, 38, 153
St. Lawrence (frigate), 92
St. Louis, 88
St. Mery, Moreau de, 51, 52
St. Paul's Catholic Church, 37, 172
St. Paul's Church, 44, 131
Salvation Army, 148
San Juan Hill, 110
Santa Maria (ship), 108
Sargeant Room, Norfolk Public Library, 10
Savannah, Americus & Montgomery Railway, 164
Sayegh, Dr. Emile S., 161
Schertzer, T. B., 110, 111
Schlitz, Shirley, 80
Schmoele, Dr. William, 142
Schneider, William, 219, 222
School of Nursing, Portsmouth General, 143

Scot, Alexander, 35
Scott, Glenn A., 217
Scott, Gen. Winfield, 87
Scott's Creek, 132, 133
Scottish Merchants, 26
Scottsville, 108, 110
Seaboard Air Line Railroad, 87, 107, 126, 165, 166, 167, 175, 178, 191
Seaboard Building, 126, 165, 172, 186
Seaboard Crest Line, 164
Seaboard Market and Armory, 121
Seaboard and Roanoke Railroad, 60, 167
Seabreeze Farms, 185
Seawall, 11, 186, 192, 196, 198, 203, 216
Seawall Art Show, 195, 206
Seawall Restaurant, 184
Seawell's Point. *See* Sewell's Point
Serapis (ship), 42, 46
Seward, Vice Mayor Raymond, 187
Sewell's Point, 102, 110
Shangri-La (aircraft carrier), 162
Shannon (British ship), 56
Sharp, Warrington, 80
Shea Terrace Elementary School, 83
Shoulder's Hill, 35
Shoulder's Hill Church, 35
Simonsdale, 174
Simpson, J. Herbert, 9, 161, 168
Singleton, William B., 88, 91
Slater, L. P., 58
Sleepy Hole Golf Course, 168
Slenderizing Salon, 179
Smith, Capt. John, 11, 18, 19, 20, 23
Smith, Kate, 152
Smith, Rachel Norcom, 70
Smith, Roy, 80
Smith, R. Irvine, 175, 186, 188, 189, 198
Snowden, Ruth, 79
South Carolina, 11, 98, 110
South Hampton Roads, 14, 15, 56, 135
South Norfolk, 174, 187
South Street, 37, 61, 114, 118, 122, 131, 139, 152
South Street Road, 117
Spanish-American War, 128, 129, 134
Spee, Adm. Graf, 136
Spong, Emily N., 75, 161, 177, 200
Spong, U.S. Sen. William B., Jr., 80, 189, 200, 203, 219, 222
Sprowle, Andrew, 26, 27, 44, 45, 92, 197
Spurling, Frankee, 9
Sterling Point Drive, 39

229

Sterling Point-Green Acres, 186
Steuart, Charles, 197
Stewart, Col. William H., 119
Stoakes, Hezekiah, 197
Stoakes, James E., 198
Stokely, Paul C., 161
Stokes, E. Anne, 9
Stokes, Emma, 59
Stokes, Dr. Ralph M., Jr., 59
Stokes, W. H. (Cap'n Billy), 59
Stone, John T., 217
Streetcars, 116, 151
Streets. *See* individual names
Stuart, Faith, 9, 217
Stuart, J. E. B. (Jeb), 98
Sturtevant, Charles H., 115
Student, The, 183
Suffolk, 14, 15, 20, 22, 45, 84, 187, 215
Suffolk Highway, 35
Suffolk Water Works, 108
Sullivan, Dennis, 112
Susan Constant (ship), 19, 21
Svetlana (frigate), 107
Sweeny, Marjorie, 79
Swimming Point, 29, 119, 133, 180
Swinburne, Capt. W. T., 94
Sycamore Hill, 35
Sycamore Hill School, 59
Sykes, Fire Chief W. B., 157

T

Taliaferro, Maj. Gen. William B., 98
Tanbark Lane, 213
Tatem, John, 31
Taylor, John, 155
Taylor, Theodore, 219, 222
Teller, Sgt. Ken, 9
Texas, 98
Texas, USS, 94, 108, 127
Thanksgiving, 21
Third Virginia Regiment, 100
Thirteenth Amendment, 99
Thomas, Philip G., 198
Thorogood (Thoroughgood, Thorowgood), 26
Tidewater Indians, 20, 21, 22, 119
Tidewater Community College, 10, 69, 70, 79, 84, 100
Tidewater Virginia, 13, 14, 15, 19, 20, 21, 43, 45, 46, 97, 108, 110
Times and Commercial Advertiser, 88
Tory, 43, 44, 45
Town Trustees, 50
Town Clock, 56
Town Hall, 56, 129, 130, 151, 172
Town Squares, 26
Trafton, William, 67

Trant, Beany, 168
Treaty of Paris, 50
Trinity Episcopal Church, 30, 36, 38, 51, 56, 104, 132, 141, 142, 172, 179
Trinity Episcopal Churchyard, 35, 46, 56, 121, 216
Trinity Episcopal Rectory, 12
Trinity Parish House, 31
Truman, President Harry S., 177
Truxton, Capt. Thomas, 136
Truxton, 135
Truxton Elementary School, 76
Tunnels, 22
Tusing, Joe, 188
Tuttle, Lt. Gen. William G. T., 219, 222
Twine, Bishop Charles A., 41
Tyler, President John, 87
Tynan, Police Chief F. T., 155

U

United Daughters of the Confederacy, 147
United States Military Academy, 58
Upper Norfolk, 22

V

Vache, the Right Reverend C. Charles, 36
Valentine Museum, Richmond, 10
Van Buren, President Martin, 87
Vass, I. G., 111
Veale, George, 197
Veale, Thomas, 31
Victory Navy Store, 158
Vietnam War, 177, 195
Virginia, CSS (USS *Merrimac*), 11, 92, 102, 103, 104, 105
Virginia, Commonwealth of, 13, 14, 15, 19, 20, 21, 22, 23, 43, 44, 45, 51, 52, 59, 60, 84, 98, 104, 107, 110, 121, 147, 176, 177
Virginia Beach, city, 15, 19, 25, 84, 185, 201
Virginia Constitutional Convention, 119
Virginia Federation of Music Clubs, 118
Virginia Guard, 98
Virginia Literary, Scientific, and Military Academy, 87
Virginia Municipal League, 198
Virginia Opera, 201
Virginia Palladium and Portsmouth Commercial Advertiser, 87
Virginia Port Authority, 167
Virginia Power, 216

Virginia Sports Hall of Fame, 9, 170
Virginia Stage Company, 201
Virginia State Library, 10
Virginia Symphony, 201
Virginia's Red Letter Year, 20
Virginian-Pilot, 10, 175

W

Walker, George C., 9
Wample, Homer, 168
Ward, Hubert, 132
Warner, John, 200
Warren, Lewis C., 161
Warren, Adm. Sir John B., 55
Washington, George, 43, 44, 46
Washington Reed House, 210
Washington (sidewheeler steamboat), 87
Washington. *See* Berkley
Washington, D. C., 56, 78, 97, 98, 107, 108, 175, 176
Washington Street, 37, 38, 48, 63, 65, 141, 157, 175
Water Street, 121, 191
Waters, Clarine Baltrip, 76
Waters, Junior High School, 76
Waters, Ruth, 76
Waters, William E., Jr., 177
Waterside, 194
Waterview, 48, 144, 173, 209
Watley, L. B., 145
Watson, Capt. Johannes, 100
Watts, A. S., 198
Watts, Col. Dempsey, 8
Watts, H. F., 140
Watts, Lee, 168
Watts, Vivian, 77
Watts, Col. Winchester, 90
Watts House, 8, 191
Waud, Alfred R., 105
Waverly Apartments, 145
Waverly Boulevard, 192
WAVY radio station and TV, 159, 169
Webb, Gloria O., 9, 198, 199
Webster, Daniel, 87
Wells, Henry, 26
Weinberg, G., Inc., Lockers/Naval Outfitters, 152
Wentz, Robert W., Jr., 9, 161
Wertenbaker, Thomas J., 110
Wesley Chapel, 36
Wesley Community Center, 39
West Indies, 51, 97
West Norfolk, 21, 113, 174, 212, 216
West Norfolk Lumber Company, 113
West Virginia, 97, 159
Western Union Office, 158
Westhaven, 173

Whipple, E. W., 198
White, Clyde, 72, 183
White, James C., 198
White, John S., 197
White, L. G., 198
White, Dr. William C., 98
Whitehead, Swepson, 58
Wiggins, Mary Frances, 79
Willet Auditorium (Willet Hall), 72
Willett, T. A., 161
William J. Davis Palace Stable, 121
Williams, Catherine, 79
Williams, Ed, 140
Williams, G. Robert, 111
Williams, Junius H., 217
Williamsburg, 15, 43, 46
Willow Oaks, 207, 213
Wilson, Esther, 120
Wilson, Holt, 58
Wilson, Willis, Esq., 45, 56
Wilson, Woodrow, 135
Wimbrough, Raymond, 74
Windows on Education (newsletter), 82
Wingfield, Rev. J. H. D., 58, 98, 99, 100, 102, 104, 105
Wingfield, Rev. John H., 31
Wood, Donna, 9
Wood, Richard, 9
Wood, Richard F., 161
Woodard, Col. Donald, 85
Woodrow Wilson High School, 64, 66, 67, 68, 72, 73, 79, 80, 170, 183, 222
Woolridge, O. B., 161
World War I, 76, 159
World War II, 73, 134, 135, 136, 137, 158, 160, 162, 166, 173
Wright, Wasena F., Jr., 10
Wright, William, 58
WSAP radio station, 159, 169
Wyatt, C. O., 140

Y

Yeats, Glenn, 203
Yellow fever epidemic, 1855, 58, 60, 97
YMCA, 124
York County, 98
York River, 15, 19
Yorktown, 11, 15, 46, 47, 51
Young, Capt. John P., 88
Young, Maudie, 9

230

about the authors

photo by William Tiernan

Alf and Ramona Mapp live at Willow Oaks, their Tidewater Georgian home on the Western Branch of the Elizabeth River, where Alf's maternal ancestors have lived for nine generations. He is an eleventh generation Virginian in both maternal and paternal descent. Ramona, born in Alabama and reared there and in Florida, moved to Tidewater in 1961 after residence in Indiana, New Mexico, Ohio, Massachusetts, and London, England.

An author and historian of international reputation, Alf holds the endowed rank of eminent professor at Old Dominion University where he has taught a variety of subjects—English, history, literature, journalism, and creative writing—since 1961. His books include *The Virginia Experiment: The Old Dominion's Role in the Making of America, Frock Coats and Epaulets, Just One Man, America Creates Its Own Literature, The Golden Dragon: Alfred the Great and His Times,* and *Thomas Jefferson: A Strange Case of Mistaken Identity,* which was a featured selection of the Book-of-the-Month Club and one of the "Forty Best Books of 1987." He is author of more than eight hundred articles in scholarly journals, popular magazines, the *New York Times,* and other metropolitan newspapers. His writings have circulated around the world in nine languages.

Ramona is professor of English at the Portsmouth Campus of Tidewater Community College, where she served for fourteen years as chair of the Division of Humanities and Social Sciences after four years on the faculty of Old Dominion University. An alumna of Indiana University, Huntingdon College, and the City Literary Institute of London, England, she received her B.A. and M.A. from Old Dominion University and her doctorate from Virginia Polytechnic Institute and State University. Her professional leadership has included program chairman of the Southeastern Conference on English in the Two-Year College and president of the South Atlantic Association of Departments of English.

Both Alf and Ramona Mapp have been active in the civic life of Portsmouth, the state, and the nation. He has chaired the Portsmouth, Virginia, American Revolution Bicentennial Commission and the Portsmouth Museums and Fine Arts Commission. He was named a National Notable of Portsmouth in 1987 and Great Citizen of Hampton Roads, and is a Commonwealth of Virginia Laureate. She has served as chair of the Portsmouth Public Library Board and president of the Tidewater Child Care Association. She received the Outstanding Professional Woman of Hampton Roads Award in 1984. Together the Mapps received the National Service Award of the Family Foundation of American in 1980. Both have played prominent roles in many cultural organizations.

Alf Mapp is included in *Who's Who in America, Who's Who in the World,* and *The National Cyclopedia of American Biography.* Ramona is in *Who's Who in the South and Southwest* and *Who's Who Among American Women.*